ESCAPE TO THE LAKES
The First Tourists

Robert Gambles

with colour photographs by Val Corbett

HAYLOFT PUBLISHING LTD
CUMBRIA

This edition published by Hayloft Publishing Ltd., 2015
First published by Bookcase, 2011

Hayloft Publishing Ltd, South Stainmore,
Kirkby Stephen, Cumbria, CA17 4DJ

tel: 07971 352473
email: books@hayloft.eu
web: www.hayloft.eu

ISBN 978 1 910237 12 0

A Catalogue record for this book is available from The British Library

Designed, printed and bound in the EU

Papers used by Hayloft are natural, recyclable products made from wood
grown in sustainable forests. The manufacturing processes conform to the
environmental regulations of the country of origin.

In memory of my wife, Hannemor,
whose love made everything possible

Mardale Green in the 1830s by Thomas Allom.
'Something worth travelling far to see' E. Lynn Linton.

Contents

Waterfall at Ambleside, J. Farrington, 1780.

PREFACE TO THE SECOND EDITION

IN writing this book I have been greatly indebted to the work of many scholars who have researched this period of the history of the Lake District, and especially to those who have painstakingly collated and edited the letters and journals, the guidebooks and notebooks, the prose and the poetry, the diaries and memoirs compiled by the curious travellers and adventurous pioneers who were among the first to make the 'tour to the Lakes'.

For those comfortable gentlefolk this was a thrilling and romantic adventure into a remote and virtually unknown corner of their country, into a wild landscape of forbidding mountains and mysterious lakes, and inhabited by rough, primitive peasants living in 'sad little huttes, only stones piled together', all quite unlike the architectural glories of Florence and Venice or the sophisticated society of Nice and Montpellier or the rugged grandeur of the Italian Alps, resorts which for several generations had been the preferred destinations of the English tourist. They did not view the fells, lakes and dales of the Lake District in the same way as later generations have learned to see them and this makes their experience of special interest in the history of tourism.

The resources of the Cumbria Library Service have been invaluable in putting together the story of these early visitors to Lakeland and I wish to express my thanks to the library staff who were unfailingly helpful guides to the relevant literature. I owe special thanks to Jackie Fay of the Local Studies Library in Kendal who took a kind personal interest in the book's progress and was of immense assistance in the search for illustrations.

All the illustrations, except those where the source is separately acknowledged, were provided by the resources of the Cumbria Library Service. Every effort has been made to acknowledge copyright and any omission is regretted.

To all those whose sketches and photographs help to enhance the book and to all those friends who contributed to the completion of the book I extend my grateful thanks.

I owe more than I can say to my beloved wife, Hannemor, who, even during her last illness, followed the progress of the work with perceptive comment and constant encouragement: I dedicate the book to her memory.

I have taken the opportunity of this new edition to make a few minor amendments but the text remains substantially unchanged. The illustrations have been reorganised and enhanced by the inclusion of a number of colour photographs by Val Corbett for which I wish to express my appreciation.

Robert Gambles, 2015

INTRODUCTION

JOHN Ruskin famously pronounced that 'Mountains are the beginning and the end of all natural scenery', a sentiment which would have seemed absurd, even incomprehensible to an earlier generation. For more than a thousand years, until the eighteenth century, mountains had been looked upon with distaste: they were described as 'Nature's shames', 'warts', 'wens', 'monstrous excrescences', 'barren deformities', 'impostumes', 'the rubbish of the earth'. Wordsworth wrote 'There is not, I believe, a single English traveller whose published writings would disprove the assertion that where precipitous rocks and mountains are mentioned at all, they are spoken of as objects of dislike and fear, and not of admiration.'

During the course of the eighteenth century all this changed. A rage for mountain scenery seized fashionable society; mountains were no longer regarded with revulsion but were spiritually uplifting and healing; a mountain scene was artistically beautiful, whether seen as a picturesque 'landskip' with the aid of a Claude glass or entirely as Nature presented it 'unimproved' by any artifice. The reasons for this change were outlined in Norman Nicholson's classic study, *The Lakers*, published in 1955, and are briefly explored in the chapters of this book.* From the 1760s a 'tour of the Lakes' – or to the mountains of Scotland or Wales – became part of the summer season for more and more of the gentry and wealthy middle class, and by 1800 Samuel Taylor Coleridge could complain, with some exaggeration, that from June to

---

* A scholarly analysis of this topic may be found in Marjorie Hope Nicholson's *Mountain Gloom and Mountain Glory*, New York 1959/1963.

September the Lake District was 'alive and swarming with tourists.' These summer visitors were numbered only in hundreds and even 50 years later barely reached 25,000, a mere trickle compared to the flood which sweeps through the Lakes each year now.

Even so, many of the features of today's tourist industry were already evident by the early nineteenth century. Tourism brought immediate benefit to the local economy: as Norman Nicholson commented, to the poverty-stricken inhabitants tourists were as welcome as Father Christmas. Many innkeepers soon became hoteliers, farmers earned badly needed income by supplying the inns, many others found employment as ostlers, coach-drivers, porters, tour-guides, and as servants in hotels and inns. Others saw opportunities to make money by providing 'tourist attractions' of various kinds, most of them with little relevance to mountain scenery or spiritual inspiration but immensely popular and financially rewarding.

Artists, too, found a highly profitable outlet for their paintings, watercolours and engravings as tourists indulged the contemporary passion for mountain scenery by buying their works either in the London galleries or in Keswick or Ambleside. Almost every artist of the time visited Lakeland to produce a portfolio of scenes to tempt tourists to take home a 'souvenir' of their tour to the Lakes.

John Ruskin considered the Lake District to be a place 'almost too beautiful to live in' and resented the arrival of the first tourists. A century later the stated purpose of the National Park is to provide opportunities for the understanding and enjoyment of the special qualities of the area for the millions of visitors who come each year.

1

WILD, BARREN AND FRIGHTFUL

THE travelling Englishman of the early eighteenth century was more familiar with France and Italy than he was with the remoter parts of his own country, and Daniel Defoe's 'wild and barren' verdict on the Lake District in the 1720s probably summarised the general impression of this little-known corner of England at that time. Edward Gibbon was told, in the hey-day of the Grand Tour, that there were 40,000 English gentry and their servants on the Continent each year. At the same time tourists were almost unknown in the Lake District. There were many reasons for this, not least of which were the exaggerated tales of the wild, primitive and even dangerous conditions prevailing there, tales spread no doubt in taverns up and down the country by the many drovers, packhorsemen and pedlars who regularly travelled to the Border counties. The region had a long history of destructive raids and invasions from Scotland, the most recent only a few years earlier when the 1745 Jacobite Rebellion sent a shudder through the whole of England. As a grisly reminder the grinning skulls of the executed rebels still remained impaled on the gates of Carlisle twenty years later.

There were also cultural and language barriers. The suspicion that those who lived in 'the North[1] were really rather rough and unrefined and had little access to fashionable culture was as firmly embedded in the southern shires then as it often is today – indeed, Jane Austen's Elizabeth Bennet declared that she even had a poor opinion of young men who lived in Derbyshire. The broad vowels of the northern counties and the even stranger

Crummock Water – T. Allom 1830s 'there is scarcely anything finer than the view from a boat in the centre of Crummock Water' (William Wordsworth)

vocabulary presented far more difficulty than French or Italian. The educated English gentleman and his lady (especially the latter) would readily have understood a reply to a very English question in France – 'Pensez-vous qu'il pleuvra aujourd'hui?' or in Italy - 'Sara una bella giornata?' but it is doubtful if they would have been enlightened by the reply to a similar enquiry given to Miss Harriet Martineau in Kentmere: 'It donks and it dozzles; and whiles it's a bit siftering; but it don't make no girt pel.'

Lakeland place-names, too, seemed alien and barbaric to the southern ear; Sizergh, Loughrigg and Watendlath did not trip off the tongue quite so smoothly as Windsor, Canterbury and Tunbridge Wells, or even Venice and Montpellier. Arthur Young felt it was necessary to apologise to the readers of his *Tour through the North of England* for the 'many barbarous and probably wrongly-spelt names' to be encountered in these parts.[1] A tour to the Lakes was a hazardous journey into the untamed wilderness, culturally outlandish and, seemingly, unrewarding.

In fact Defoe had avoided central Lakeland. Soon after leaving Lancaster he cast his eyes on the mountains ahead and fearfully noting that they were 'high and formidable' and 'had a kind of unhospitable terror in them', he turned away to Kirkby Stephen and the Eden Valley.[2] There were others, however, made of sterner stuff who braved the mountain wilderness but their descriptions did nothing to persuade their readers that there was anything here to divert them from the fashionable trek to the Alps or the comfortable Assembly Rooms of Bath.

Nor did the gloomy reports of the Lakeland weather encourage folk to turn away from the blue skies of the Mediterranean: James Clarke in 1787 had warned that even on a clear day 'a black cloud will start up instantly from behind a mountain, and if you are not near a house, ten to one you are wet before you can run a hundred yards' and William Hutchinson related how their enjoyment of the view from the summit of Skiddaw was suddenly interrupted by a violent burst of thunder which 'stunned our senses' and caused their guide to 'lay upon the earth terrified and amazed.' Even Wordsworth had to admit that Lakeland 'is, indeed, subject to much bad weather, and it has been ascertained that twice as much rain falls here as in many parts of the island.'[3]

Guidebooks and journals of the eighteenth century described the mountain scenery of Lakeland in such terms as to deter all but the most intrepid tourist: prospective travellers were warned to expect 'vast precipices', 'rocks twice the height of St Paul's', 'chasms of near a thousand yards deep', 'cliffs of stupendous height . . . where mortal foot never yet approached.' The Yorkshire topographer, Ralph Thoresby, had set the tone as early as 1697 when he found the Lake District 'full of horrors: dreadful fells, hideous wastes, horrid waterfalls, terrible rocks and ghastly precipices.'[4] No place for faint-hearts.

Celia Fiennes, a young 'lady of quality', journeying 'through England on a side-saddle' in the 1690s, had already portrayed a discouraging picture of the district. She thought the mountains were 'very terrible' and the land 'desert and barren' with only tiny fields able to grow 'barley, oates, beans and lentils, noe wheat or rhye for they are so cold . . . they cannot venture on that sort of tillage,' and the poor people lived in 'sad little huttes . . . only stones piled together, no mortar or plaster within or without.' Other travellers commented on the unhealthy diet of dried salted meat and bread made from oatmeal instead of the richer wheaten bread which furnished the tables of the wealthy in the south.

Equally discouraging were reports of the shortcomings in the accommodation to be expected in this backward region: The

Dunmail Raise – J. Harwood 1842 'wild, barren and frightful'
(Daniel Defoe)

Buttermere Hause – J. Harwood 1842 'terrible rocks and ghastly precipices' (R. Thoresby)

Honourable Mrs Murray in 1796 had written that in Patterdale she had been 'obliged to pass the night in a chair by the kitchen fire, there not being a bed in the house fit to put myself upon,' and even in 1818 John Keats and his companion spent a restless night at the Nag's Head Inn at Wythburn because 'there were so many fleas in the beds.'[5]

Nor were the inhabitants and their way of life any more appealing to the educated classes of the time. Religious ignorance, it seems, was widespread and in Cumberland most of the people could not say the Lord's Prayer, while John Norden, topographer and royal surveyor, reported that in the 'great and spacious wastes, mountains and heaths... the people (are) given to little or no kind of labour, living very hardly with oaten bread, sour whey, and goats' milk... and are as ignorant of God or of any civil course of life as the very savages among the infidels.'[6] Several generations later a Victorian guide book seemed to suggest that very little had changed: 'The simple, but somewhat rough, manners of the Westmorland and Cumbrian peasantry have not undergone any material change from their increased intercourse with the world; and education has had hitherto little effect in refining their tastes, elevating their character or improving their minds'[7] – but by that time tourists were visiting the Lakes in their thousands and had discovered that the 'peasantry' there were no more 'uneducated' and 'unrefined' than those in the rest of the country, and were honest, hard-working and hospitable country folk, living in one of the most spectacularly beautiful and spiritually rewarding landscapes in England.

One of the most important factors in the development of tourism is the provision of good travelling and transport facilities. In the first half of the eighteenth century Cumberland and Westmorland had the worst roads in the country, most of them no more than rough bridleways just wide enough to accommodate the packhorse trains or the two-wheeled carts which used them. Almost everyone travelled on horseback. Celia Fiennes in 1698 was dismayed even by the condition of the road from Lancaster to Kendal which she described as 'stony and steep, far worse than the Peake in Derbyshire' and by the road from Kendal to Bowness which was extremely narrow and not capable of taking carriages. High Constable Benjamin Browne of Townend, Troutbeck, in his Survey of Roads in 1730-31, reported that all the roads in the Kendal area were in a bad state and were 'very narrow' and 'much covered with ye hedges', and forty years later Arthur Young gave this blunt warning to anyone who was contemplating a tour of the Lakes: 'Let me seriously caution all travellers who may accidentally propose to travel this terrible country, to avoid it as they would the devil, for a thousand to one they may break their necks or their limbs, or overthrows or breakings down. They will meet here with ruts four feet deep and floating with mud.'[8]

By 1770, however, roads were improving and there were many who considered the odds quoted by Young promised more of an adventure than a threat: as a modern historian wrote – 'Those travellers brave enough to risk life and limb came expecting the worst and were seldom disappointed.'[9] A mood of national confidence was emerging with a flourishing economy and spectacular successes on land and sea against both the French and the Spanish and this, paradoxically, helped to create a deeper interest in and curiosity about Britain itself, and especially the 'unexplored' parts of the country. For the first time remote and mountainous areas were no longer regarded as full of horror and frightfulness but as wholesome and spiritually healing, 'the highest form of natural beauty and a reminder of God's sublimity.'[10]

2

A WHOLE GENERATION OF GENTLEFOLK TOOK TO THE ROAD

IT is one of the better known facts of English history that during their 400-year occupation of this country the Romans created a fine network of well-constructed roads. It is equally true that in the 1,300 years between the departure of the Legions and the eighteenth century very little was done to maintain these roads and virtually nothing was achieved either in road building or in improved methods of construction. Those who travelled did so on horseback, goods were conveyed by horse-drawn cart or by packhorse. Roads became very little more than dirt tracks with no surface other than loose stones occasionally used to fill the worst potholes, muddy and deeply rutted in winter and little better in summer.

Daniel Defoe, travelling in Lancashire in the 1720s, described the main road as 'paved with small pebbles' and about one and a half yards wide. It was almost impossible for a horseman to pass a packhorse train on this narrow causeway, a poor shadow of its Roman predecessor which had a metalled surface and had a width of seven yards. For most of the Middle Ages these inadequate roads were no great inconvenience but by the early eighteenth century trade was increasing rapidly and with the first stirrings of the Industrial Revolution national economic development was beginning to demand a more efficient system of transport.

For many centuries the maintenance of roads and bridges had been the responsibility of the parish, an arrangement much resented by the parishioners who had to give six days a year unpaid labour towards the repair and maintenance of roads passing through their parish, roads largely used by travellers from other parts of the country. Reform of local government seemed impossible to achieve and so the government turned to private enterprise to bring about the much-needed improvement in the country's roads. Turnpike Trusts were given Parliamentary powers to improve and maintain an approved stretch of road and to erect toll-gates where payment could be demanded for the right to travel along that section of the road.

The first Turnpike Trust was established in 1706 but not a great deal was accomplished in the next 40 years. As so often in our history it required a direct threat to national security to provide the spur to action. In 1745 the Jacobite army of Prince Charles Stuart captured Carlisle and advanced unchecked to within little more than 100 miles of London before the capital was aware of their progress. The Duke of Cumberland's pursuit of the retreating

Wagon and horses by a cottage in Patterdale – P. J. Loutherbourg, 1787 – Celia Fiennes 'sad little huttes' (crown copyright).

rebels was so hindered by the dreadful state of the roads, especially between Kendal and Penrith, that a seriously alarmed Establishment embarked on a nationwide frenzy of turnpike construction. Between 1750 and 1772 the total length of turnpike roads was increased from 2,000 miles to 15,000 miles and Cumbria, which had been largely neglected until after the '45 Rebellion, was endowed not only with a number of turnpikes within the Lake District itself, but major turnpikes were converging on the area from north, east, south and west. They were described by the *Gentleman's Magazine* as 'equal to the best Turnpikes around London'. Kendal and Keswick could now be reached by mostly completed turnpikes from Preston and Lancaster, from Whitehaven and Carlisle, from Yorkshire and from Newcastle.

By the 1770s travellers could proceed on completed sections of generally good turnpike roads from either Keswick or Kendal to Grasmere, Ambleside, Windermere and even Penrith. The notorious route over Shap, which had been described as 'nothing

The Nags Head, Wythburn – 'post horses, mountain ponies and guides...
from it may be made the shortest ascent of Helvellyn'
from an advertisement, Rev. G. Darrall.

Coach on the road by Skiddaw – P. J. Loutherbourg, 1787. Skiddaw – 'the Etna of the North, 1500 yards high.' (crown copyright).

but bogs and mires and the tops of high hills' where the armies of both Charles Stuart and the Duke of Cumberland had struggled to make headway, now carried a regular mail and stagecoach service. The first stagecoach, drawn by six horses and optimistically named 'The Flying Machine', went over Shap in 1763 and by the 1780s the Lake District was equipped with almost 400 miles of newly constructed turnpikes. Nationally, turnpike construction was often piecemeal, but even so the journey time for passenger coaches from London to Kendal had been reduced from nine days in 1734 to three days in 1773, and by 1825 the 300 miles could, given good weather and no breakdowns, be covered in 24-36 hours.[1]

A journey to the Lake District was no longer an undertaking necessarily fraught with a variety of perils and much discomfort; nor was the lake and mountain scenery graphically described by the writers of guidebooks and journals so difficult to reach or so formidably 'alpine' to behold as the painters and engravers were so busily portraying it.

Travelling had been made much less hazardous not only by improved roads but also by the certainty of a coaching inn with a warm fire and a hearty meal at the end of a day's journey and by the disappearance of the highwaymen who had terrorised and robbed travellers of the previous generation: Dick Turpin and his ilk no longer haunted the lonely roads with their demand to 'Stand and Deliver' or came 'riding, riding up to the old inn door'. Long journeys had also become less physically exhausting with improvements in coach-building techniques. Those lucky and wealthy enough to have inside seats on the stagecoach now enjoyed the comfort of padded upholstery and all appreciated the introduction of steel springs (and by 1830 rubber 'shock absorbers') to cushion the jolts of uneven road surfaces. Travel began to seem much less perilous and discouraging and could even be an exciting and pleasurable adventure.

The first essential for the development of Lakeland tourism was now in place: accessibility via reasonable roads and the provision of regular and more comfortable means of transport. By the end of the eighteenth century a network of roads and scheduled coach services was firmly established. In 1800 passengers passing through the turnpike tollgate at Troutbeck Bridge, between Windermere and Ambleside, were numbered in hundreds only; fifty years later this had increased to 21,480 of whom 15,420 went on to Grasmere and Keswick. The great majority of these early tourists would have to be sufficiently wealthy to own private coaches or to afford the high cost of such a journey and the expenses of accommodation and hiring guides, horses and carriages within the Lake District. Thus they were, for the most part, drawn from the upper classes of society or from the *nouveaux riches* of the new industrial middle class who had both the money and the ambition to emulate the gentry. As Norman Nicholson put it: 'A whole generation of gentlefolk took to the roads.'[2]

Not all travellers chose to use the new turnpike to Kendal to make their way to the heart of the Lake District: the road from Kendal to Windermere was in poor condition and, as a lady's journal of c1830 vividly relates, it was, even at that date, a route fraught with danger. As her carriage hurtled and swayed down a particularly steep hill, 'We did not scream,' she says, 'but clung to each other.'[3] Many preferred to take the ancient 'highway' across the sands of Morecambe Bay from Hest Bank, near Lancaster, to Ulverston. A regular passenger and freight service was maintained until 1857 when Lancaster and Ulverston were linked by rail. In 1781 the *Cumberland Pacquet* carried an advertisement for a diligence that departed from the 'Sun Inn at Lancaster every Monday, Wednesday and Friday, as the tide will permit, to Ulverston over the sands.' The fare was five shillings and the journey took two hours. Larger coaches carrying up to fifteen passengers also ran a regular service over the sands to Ulverston and on to Bowness to join the new (1760s) turnpike to Ambleside, Grasmere and Keswick.

One important advantage of the 'sands crossing' was that it was more than twenty miles shorter to Ulverston than the packhorse route via Kendal and even sixteen miles less than the new (1818) turnpike via Levens Bridge. The hard sand surface also ensured a much smoother ride than could be enjoyed by road. The disadvantages were many but in days when it was accepted that to travel at all was to face any number of possible hazards these were not regarded as a serious deterrent but rather as a new and exciting experience. The channels of the Rivers Keer and Kent had to be forded and these were constantly changing; quicksands and deep holes could appear to trap the unwary, swallowing people and overturning carts and coaches; times of tides had to be closely observed as the incoming tide races in as a wall of water several feet high and moving faster than a man can run.

Stagecoaches at Wythburn – photographer unknown.

The monks of Conishead and Cartmel Priories had provided guides across these treacherous reaches in medieval times and after the dissolution this responsibility was transferred to the Duchy of Lancaster. Even so accidents and drownings were not uncommon and very many lives were lost over the years: the Registers of Cartmel Priory alone record a total of 141 drownings in the 300 years before 1880. The early tourists to the Lake District appear to have regarded these possible hazards as a thrilling introduction to their tour of Lakeland, the sense of danger giving, as one writer put it 'something of the piquancy of adventure to the journey.'

Ann Radcliffe, the author of gothic novels, wrote a lyrical account of her early morning crossing of the sands; Adam Walker described the journey as a ride on a 'road more even than a gravel walk in a garden,' admired the view of the coastline, and casually related that he had made the crossing 'when we were obliged to open the two doors of the chaise and let the water run through... a singular but not unpleasant ride.' The Honourable Mrs Sarah Murray, while admitting that the hard surface gave a smooth and quiet ride, was distinctly apprehensive about the whole enterprise, fearfully noting that 'should any unforeseen accident happen to your carriage or your horses while on the sands the sea might return and overwhelm you before you could escape.' Thomas Gray, characteristically, made preliminary enquiries about the danger involved, but in his two crossings he was apparently too fascinated by the contrasting landscapes and seascapes to worry unduly about the potential perils. Thomas West regarded the journey as 'of little more danger than any other... On a fine day there is not a more pleasant sea-side journey in the Kingdom.' William Green, who edited West's *Guide to the Lakes*, felt it necessary to modify this enthusiasm by reminding the traveller that he should rather bear in mind that the 'retreated ocean' is lurking on the

Stage-wagon from 1805.

horizon and that 'but a few hours before the whole expanse was covered with some fathoms of water, and that in a few more it will as certainly be covered again.'

Wordsworth assures 'the stranger' that 'from the moment he sets his foot on those Sands, he seems to leave the turmoil and traffic of the world behind him; and, crossing the majestic plain whence the sea has retired, he beholds... the cluster of mountains among which he is going to wander, and towards whose recesses... he is gradually and peacefully led,' sentiments far more reassuring to the tourist than the gloomy comments by such as John Briggs who declared that he 'did not relish the idea of drowning; it would make a disagreeable opening to our adventure' or the oft repeated tale of a guide's reply when he was asked if anyone was ever lost on the sands, 'I never knew any lost,' said the guide, 'there's one or two drowned now and then, but they're generally found somewhere when th'tide goes out.'[4]

We may be reasonably sure that the guides who accompanied the early tourists across the sands, like tourist guides everywhere, entertained their captive guests with well-rehearsed tales of every grim and spine-chilling disaster in the long history of this popular and exhilarating route into the mountain fastnesses of Lakeland.[5] By whichever route they came the wealthy and leisured classes had by the 1770s 'discovered' the Lake District. Compared to the torrent of tourists who pour into the area today – or even to the summer weekend invasions of Keswick and Windermere brought by the new railways – the eighteenth century produced only a trickle. They were the affluent members of society many of whom would normally have considered the Grand Tour of France and Italy as an appropriate 'cultural experience', but this option was virtually closed during the long periods of European warfare in the late eighteenth and early nineteenth centuries. Thus it was that William Wilberforce, a frequent visitor to the Lake District, could

Cockle gatherers on Leven Sands 'the famousest cockles of all England'
(Edmund Sandford).

write that 'the banks of the Thames are scarcely more public than those of Windermere,' that Peter Crosthwaite could boast that, in 1793, 1,540 of the 'nobility and gentry' visited his eccentric museum in Keswick, and that the proprietor of the Salutation Inn in Ambleside found it profitable to keep six 'four-in-hand' coaches and 90 horses available for hire to his guests. The 'Lakers' had arrived.[6]

3

ITH NEAME O'FACKINS, WOT A BROUGHTIN YOA HERE?*

IN the second half of the eighteenth century a vogue for mountain scenery swept through the upper classes of England. Mountains, which in earlier centuries had been despised as 'deformities', 'monstrous excrescences', 'the rubbish of the earth', now became objects of admiration; 'no longer repugnant, they had become the highest form of natural beauty and a reminder of God's sublimity' and 'the inhabitants of mountain areas ceased to be universally despised for their barbarism; instead they were praised for their innocence and simplicity'.[1] But, like the Alps, these British mountains had to be viewed from a safe distance, preferably with the assistance of a Claude glass[2] to create a framed 'picturesque' scene and soften the 'horror' of the gaping abyss and precipitous crag.

Artists flocked to Lakeland to produce paintings, watercolours, and engravings of such scenes, distinguished by their improbable Alpine 'grandeur', and found a highly profitable market in the London galleries. This played a significant part in stimulating tourist interest in the Lake District. Few of these visitors, however, gave a thought to the possibility of setting foot on the

---

*Budworths attempt at Cumbrian dialect may be roughly translated as 'What in God's (or the Devil's) name brought you up here? I never come except to find a lost sheep, and then I'm so angry with it I could throw it down the pike.'

'precipitous' slopes or scaling the 'awesome' crags. They came, rather, to enjoy the thrill of experiencing wild natural 'beauty lying in the lap of horror', all viewed on guided tours of picturesque 'stations'. Joseph Budworth, in 1792, was the first author of a travel journal to describe the pleasures to be gained by a not too challenging climb to the summits of the Lakeland fells, and where he pointed the way others eventually followed. By the first decades of the nineteenth century the paths to the summits of Skiddaw, Helvellyn and Great Gable were trodden by more delicate feet than those of the local shepherds who guided them.

Budworth's guide on his expedition to Pike of Stickle was a young Langdale shepherd boy, Paul Postlethwaite, who was totally mystified why anyone should wish to climb up there for no obvious reason, and was driven to ask 'Ith neame o'fackins, wot a broughtin yoa here? ...I neor cum here but after runnaway sheop, an I'm then so vext at urn, I cud throa un deawn th' Poike'.* Budworth's reply, 'Curiosity, Paul,' encapsulates the spirit of the age and helps to an understanding of the Georgian enthusiasm for the long journey to the Lake District.[3]

The reign of George III was an age of curiosity when old conventions and habits of mind began to be challenged by a flood of scientific and mechanical inventions, and by radical social and political philosophies which affected almost every aspect of life, some of which found a ready response among the educated old upper and new middle classes of society. Experiments in methods of agriculture, discoveries in industrial processes, new sources of power, innovations in food, dress, social customs, literature, architecture and art – all these and, in the wake of events in America and France, radical, even revolutionary, political theories – excited the curiosity of these restless decades, and an unprecedented outpouring of magazines, newspapers and journals helped to disseminate them. There was also a sea-change in the conventional view of the relationship between man and nature: hitherto the Book of Genesis had been the basis of a belief that all the natural world had been created for the use of man (Genesis i 26-29; ix 2-3); by the mid-eighteenth century a new theology had begun to emerge which proclaimed that God's design was perfect and that all living creatures – man, trees, plants, birds and animals – were part of an ecological chain and each had its own purpose and perfection of design. The natural world was now to be admired not despised or subjugated.

Theology and science soon came together to marvel at the beauty of God's Creation and it became fashionable to study nature for its own sake, to seek out, observe, sketch, categorise, name and wonder at all natural life.[4]

This flurry of social, scientific and intellectual change was accompanied by an unprecedented rate of growth of industry and of the urban population. London's population doubled from 700,000 in the mid-eighteenth century to almost 1,500,000 by 1830 and many other towns experienced similar expansion. Unfortunately, little was done to improve the medieval arrangements for sanitation and access to clean water. Neither sewers nor water supplies were provided for all the additional houses which were built. Cesspools, open ditches and the cellars of houses were soon full to overflowing and the Thames itself was a stinking sewer. Added to the human detritus were the deposits of hundreds of cattle, sheep and pigs which were driven through the streets to markets or to the slaughterhouses, and the 200 tons of manure left in their wake every day by 100,000 horses. And drifting over almost every street were the foul-smelling odours from tanneries, fishmongers, butchers and skinners mingled with the nauseating stink of rotting meat, fruit and vegetables.

Life in the capital has been pithily described as 'an intolerable rookery of humanity established on a dunghill'.[5] The all-pervading stench which filled the air was so well portrayed in Henry Mayhew's *London* that a modern writer suggests that 'just to read it could leave the reader overwhelmed and exhausted' and ready 'squeamishly to pull out his handkerchief'.[6] These appalling conditions which caused so much ill-health drove those who had the means to escape to the wholesome fresh air and pure spring water of the hilly regions.

The Malverns, the Welsh mountains, the Derbyshire Peak, the Highlands of Scotland, the Lake District, all welcomed these refugees from the urban smoke and squalor.

The developing appreciation of nature and of wild, untamed, mountainous regions was driven by more than a wish to escape the noisome atmosphere of the towns. It is difficult for us today fully to understand the profound shock experienced by so many in England at the transformation of the landscape brought about by the agricultural enclosures. A wide open countryside of heath, commons and unfenced field systems was replaced within a lifetime by uniform, rectangular enclosures.

Two million acres of land which had not hitherto been cultivated as arable or pasture were enclosed and brought under the plough and a further two million acres of land already in agricultural use were also divided into regular fields enclosed by hedges and walls. William Gilpin found these 'formalities of hedgerow trees and square divisions of property disgusting to a high degree' while William Pearson ruefully chronicled in his *Journals* the disappearance of almost all the rich and varied wildlife as the waste and wetlands of his beloved Lyth Valley were drained, hedged and fenced and brought into cultivation. John Stuart Mill, in a passage which would be strikingly apt in a modern conservation tract, declared that there was no 'satisfaction in contemplating a world with . . . all quadrupeds or birds which are not domesticated for man's use exterminated . . . every hedgerow or superfluous tree rooted out, and scarcely a place left where a wild shrub or flower could grow without being eradicated as a weed in the name of improved agriculture.'[7]

The urge to travel to the wild, untamed mountains which seized so many of the early tourists was thus partly stimulated by a romantic nostalgia for a world they had already lost or which was fast disappearing before their eyes. William Gilpin assured his many readers that England was 'more beautiful in a state of nature than in a state of cultivation.'[8]

Artists tempted potential visitors by their representation of the Cumbrian mountains in the 'Alpine' style of Claude, Poussin or Salvator Rosa, while Thomas West (following Hutchinson's *Excursion to the Lakes*) deftly led his readers from the 'delicate touches of Claude' at Coniston to 'the noble scenes of Poussin' at Windermere and on to the 'stupendous romantic ideas of Salvator Rosa' by Derwentwater.[9]

However adventurous and curious they may feel, most tourists of any generation find confidence with a guidebook in hand. The first 'tourists' were pioneers venturing into virtually unknown lands, but from the 1770s visitors to the Lakes can no longer be described as 'explorers'; some twenty guidebooks were published between 1770 and 1820, varying greatly in quality and emphasis, but cumulatively, as Norman Nicholson lamented, changing tourism in the Lakes from a journey of discovery to a planned itinerary visiting designated beauty spots like exhibits at a flower show; pandering to the fashionable search for the picturesque, visitors were told where to go, how to get there and what to see on arrival:

'Tourists were no longer pioneers or explorers, they were holi-day-makers. Curiosity became a mere itch for oddities, the artist's careful assessment of the landscape in terms of visual beauty and design becomes a mere taste for prettiness; the re-search of historians becomes a mere eye for a monument and an ear for a legend; and the genuine virtuosity of sensual response becomes a mere search for thrills.'[10]

All this, however, is in the very nature of tourism and the writers of guidebooks found an eager market. The first 'authentic' guide-book, Thomas West's *Guide to the Lakes in Cumberland, West-morland and Lancashire* published in 1778, enjoyed immense popularity and reached its tenth edition in 1812. West not only set out convincing reasons why a tour to the Lake District was a rewarding experience but directed his readers to a series of view-points, or 'stations' with a detailed description of what to look for. William Gilpin's *Observations,* a two-volume offering in 1786, went to a third edition within six years; Joseph Budworth's *Fortnight's Ramble to the Lakes* of 1792 had a second edition only three years later; Wordsworth's famous *Guide* appeared in 1810 and was published with numerous changes no less than eight times in the poet's own lifetime.

Just as many of today's fell walkers may be seen with a Wain-wright Guide in one hand and a digital camera in the other, so their predecessors in late Victorian times would be equipped with Baddeley and a brandy flask, and their Georgian forebears with West and a Claude glass. The mountains were no longer full of horrors; on the contrary, they were now beautiful and spiritually uplifting, and the guidebooks did much to encourage the landed gentry and the prosperous urban industrialists to share the enthu-siasm of Jane Austen's Elizabeth Bennet at the prospect of a tour to Lakeland: 'What hours of transport we shall spend! And when we do return. . . we will know where we have gone - we will recollect what we have seen. Lakes, mountains, and rivers, shall not be jumbled together in our imaginations. . .'[11] She probably already had West and Wordsworth on her reading list. What a loss to the literature of Lakeland it was that she never made the journey!

One further asset was needed to convert the adventurers of the 1750s and 60s into the tourists of the 1790s and 1800s. Maps of the Lake District produced before the middle of the eighteenth century were sadly lacking in detail and accuracy but in response to the new tourism the first detailed maps began to appear, most of them still with bewildering inaccuracies, faults which were perpetuated as publishers copied from one another in the rush to

The Vale of St John – G. Pickering 1833. 'A most singularly interesting assemblage of the wild and the lovely' (W. Green)

profit from the expanding market. A number of maps issued in the 1760s and 1770s became notorious for indicating the existence of a highway from Wrynose Pass over Crinkle Crags, Bow Fell and Esk Pike to Wasdale Head, and even for wrongly depicting the lakes.

The first detailed maps, with fewer inaccuracies than their predecessors, were published in the 1770s by Thomas Jefferys, Geographer to the King, and Thomas Donald, both showing clearly the new turnpike roads and other passable routes as well as many place names and a useful delineation of the fells. In subsequent years maps appeared in great profusion, many being little more than copies or revised versions of Jefferys and Donald, but it was an eccentric entrepreneur from Keswick who realised that what tourists really needed were detailed maps of the picturesque beauty spots on their guidebook itineraries. Between 1783 and 1794 Peter Crosthwaite published a series of remarkably accurate maps of the major lakes on the scale of three inches to the mile showing the various roads round the lakes, Thomas West's 'stations' (and a few of his own), all decorated with sketches of local features likely to be of interest to tourists. Crosthwaite, who styled himself 'Guide, Pilot, Geographer and Hydrographer to the Nobility and Gentry who make the Tour to the Lakes', claimed to have sold many thousands of his maps to visitors to his Keswick Museum.[12]

Spurred on by curiosity; inspired by a spirit of adventure and a search for 'the new'; secure in the belief that the country was now at last settled and free from fear of civil, dynastic and religious strife; encouraged by the greater comfort of travel on the new turnpikes and in their sprung and upholstered coaches; eager to see for themselves the dramatic mountain scenes portrayed by so many of the nation's distinguished artists; hopeful of a sight of the celebrated 'Lake Poets'; instilled with all the ardour and sentiments of the 'Romantic Movement'; happy to escape for a while the stifling air and debilitating life of the capital; armed with the latest guidebooks and equipped with Crosthwaite's maps, the early nineteenth century tourist had every reason to look forward to a tour of the lakes as 'rapturously' as Miss Elizabeth Bennet.

4

NOT CORRECTLY PICTURESQUE

THE twentieth century Oxford historian, David Ogg, once aptly described the eighteenth century as 'the age when wealth and leisure enabled a small minority to achieve a level in the amenities of life unequalled either before or since, a high standard of civilisation which stimulated the architect, the sculptor, the painter and the musician to creative work which conformed, not to the opinion of the many, but to the taste of an educated few'.[1] These few were the upper classes of a socially rigidly divided society – the titled, landowning aristocracy comprised of some 300 families, and, decidedly below them in the social order but not always inferior in worldly wealth, the 3,000 or so families of

Derwentwater and Lowdore – H. Gastineau, 1833.

landed gentry who were, in turn, careful to assert their social superiority to the educated, influential but largely landless and rarely wealthy professional class of lawyers, doctors, clergymen and academics, and below them again, in social status if not in wealth, the nouveau riche middle class of industrial entrepreneurs.[2]

The small number of aristocratic families owned one-quarter of all the land in England and at the time only they could contemplate the vast expenditure involved in a six or twelve months grand tour on the Continent. They may have been temporarily 'exiled' from their Grand Tour of Switzerland, France and Italy by the frequent wars between 1740 and 1815 but they were quick to return whenever peace was restored.[3] They were unlikely to consider a tour to the Lake District as an acceptable alternative: here there were no grand chateaux or palazzi to rent nor gatherings of social equals to entertain – 'We are now *(only)* 38 at table' lamented Georgiana Spencer's grandmother in Spa after the Spencer parents had departed for a tour of Italy.[4] Nor could the Lake District offer an almost inexhaustible array of great architecture, art, music, street carnivals and other excitements of cosmopolitan urban life. Keswick was no Venice; Ambleside no Montpellier. In Grasmere one day in 1800 Dorothy Wordsworth noted that 'a coronetted landau went by', but this must have been a rare event worthy of recording in her Journals.[5]

It was from their tours of Europe that the English aristocracy acquired the artistic tastes which led them to adorn their new country mansions with artwork (genuine or spurious) brought home from Italy and France, notably sculpture and pictures of Alpine scenery by Claude Lorraine, Salvator Rosa and Nicholas Poussin. This vogue was quickly taken up by the gentry and the more ambitious among the emerging middle class whose social aspirations seemed to demand that they take the gentry as their

Buttermere lake and village – G. Pickering, 1833.

exemplars. The most affluent aristocrats were erecting imposing stately mansions set in vast acres of landscaped parkland; Lakeland was soon dotted with the solid country houses of successful bankers, brewers, textile manufacturers, lawyers, civil servants, surgeons, headmasters and churchmen. English artists, engravers, water-colourists and painters in oil flocked to the Lake District to meet the demand for pictures of mountain scenery in the style of the European artists.

In the half century before 1800 almost all the leading artists and engravers made the journey to Lakeland to produce often substantial portfolios of mountain scenes which found a ready market at handsome prices.[6] Among the first was William Bellers whose paintings were widely sold as high quality engravings and did much to publicise the Lake District and encourage others to follow in his footsteps. By 1800 such eminent artists as Thomas Gainsborough, J. M. W. Turner, J. B. de Loutherbourg, Joseph Farington and John Glover had joined this lucrative enterprise and they were soon followed, among many others, by John Constable, J. B. Pyne, Peter de Wint, William Westall and Paul Sandby Munn. The founding of the Society for the Painting of Watercolours in 1805 brought further publicity to the Lake District and financial rewards to the artists. Almost 400 paintings of the area were exhibited in the first years of the society's existence, 'Before the end of the eighteenth century not only were the techniques of engraving, etching and mezzotint at their height in Britain, but the use of the stippling process and, a little later, the substitution of steel plates for copper, were giving new facilities for the art of book illustration'.[7] The Lakeland illustrations of Thomas Allom, William Green, Joseph Farington, T. L. Aspland, T. H. A. Fielding and William Westall are still among the finest ever produced. Galleries were opened in Keswick and Ambleside to sell these prints to tourists and did a flourishing trade.

The 'discovery' and appeal of mountain scenery in the eighteenth century was closely related to the contemporary tradition of European painting. The very term 'landscape' was used because the scene was reminiscent of 'landskip' painting; and such a scene was 'picturesque' because it resembled a picture. For much of the eighteenth century the influence of Claude, Poussin and Salvator Rose was all-pervading: English artists portrayed the modest Lake District fells as steep, craggy and forbiddingly Alpine, set in classically composed pictures. Guide books written in the second half of the eighteenth century constantly refer to the work of these foreign artists as the medium by which mountain scenery is to be interpreted. John Brown in 1767 claimed that an appreciation of the landscape in the Vale of Keswick 'would require the united powers of Claude, Salvator and Poussin'; and William Gilpin's conviction that landscape should be seen as compositions of artificially contrived views is directly derived from the paintings of these 'Alpine' artists. Even Wordsworth who, as one might expect, was much opposed to the whole concept of the 'picturesque', was impelled to observe on the view of Rydal Falls that 'whatever Salvator might desire could there be found'.[9] All these comments were clearly addressed to a public well acquainted with the work of these Continental artists – the wealthy and educated few.

Thomas West's *Guide* (1778) and William Gilpin's *Observations . . . on the Lakes* (1786), confirmed this cult of the picturesque as the predominant tourist attraction in the first 50 years of Lakeland tourism. Gilpin has been described as 'the apostle of the picturesque'.[10] As far as he was concerned Nature could not be relied upon to present a truly artistic landscape scene: 'This view,' Gilpin pronounced, 'I should not scruple to call correctly picturesque; which is seldom the character of a purely natural scene.'[11] All mountains, lakes and waterfalls, he added, had 'deformities' which 'a practised eye would wish to correct.'[12]

Thomas West, having directed his readers to selected 'stations'

Claife Station, Windermere, R. Ackermann, 1820. Thomas West's first viewing 'station' on Windermere comprising 'all the beauties of the lake'.

41

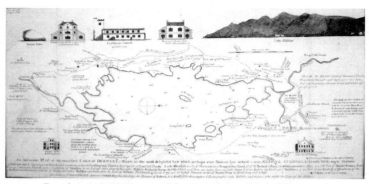

Crosthwaite's 1811 map of the 'match less lake of Derwent'.

at various points of the Lake District, then gave detailed instructions how to obtain the most 'picturesque' views. Derwentwater, for example, had eight stations from which the visitor could experience, especially if suitably equipped with a Claude glass, a series of artistic gems – a pastime which the modern tourist with his camera and picture postcards enthusiastically continues.

By 1800 tourists were travelling to the Lake District in increasing numbers all in search of the picturesque, a cult which attracted a challenge from the emerging Romantic Movement, notably from Wordsworth for whom Nature needed no improvement or artistic adjustment but rather an appreciation of the 'sense sublime of something more deeply interfused' and a willingness to hear 'the still, sad music of humanity.' Satirists also had their day: James Plumtre, a Fellow of Clare College, Cambridge, wrote a comic opera in which Miss Veronica Beccabunga, complete with Claude glass, demonstrates a picturesque composition she has discovered, explaining that 'If it is not like what it is, it is like what it ought to be. I have only made it picturesque.' Even more popular was 'The Tour of Dr Syntax in search of the picturesque,' a satire in verse on the craze for the picturesque and on the guidebooks which fostered it:

> 'I'll make a Tour and then I'll write it;
> I'll ride and write and sketch and print
> And thus create a real mint,
> I'll prose it here and verse it there
> And picturesque it everywhere'[13]

The Romantic Movement added a new dimension to contemporary appreciation of the countryside. For Wordsworth, as for John Clare, the disappearance of the open landscape of the English rural scene as the hedges, walls and fences of enclosed agriculture spread across the country was a national disaster, a violation of nature's integrity and depriving mankind of the spiritual resource needed for personal fulfilment. When Shelley cried 'I love all waste and solitary places' he was echoing the feelings of many of his generation who deplored the loss of so much uncultivated

Windermere Lake from the Ferry House, T. Allom, 1833.

Castle Crag, Borrowdale, T. Allom, 1833

and unenclosed countryside and the rapid growth of industrial towns.

The wild mountain regions were now seen as havens of solitude and tranquillity, places where humanity could escape the pressures and unhealthy environment of urban life and experience a moral uplift and a reinvigoration of the wilting spirit. John Stuart Mill neatly summarised this in his *Principles of Political Economy*: 'Solitude in the presence of natural beauty and grandeur is the cradle of thoughts and aspirations which are not only good for the individual, but which society could ill do without.'[14] By 1800 a few Lakeland visitors began to seek and find this solitude by climbing the fells where, at the time, they were unlikely to be disturbed by more than a Herdwick sheep.

This new appreciation of mountain scenery did not replace the search for the 'picturesque': there have always been those who come to exclaim at the grandeur of the Lakeland scene with an eye only for the 'picturesque' beauty spot, but from the early nine-teenth century they have existed side by side with those who come to commune with nature and to experience 'the joy of ele-vated thoughts' and

> that blessed mood,
> In which the heavy and the weary weight
> Of all this unintelligible world,
> Is lightened.[15]

5

MANY FLEAS WERE IN THE BEDS

THE millions of tourists who visit the Lake District each year may be reasonably certain that when they arrive at their hotel, inn or farmhouse accommodation, they will find their rooms and their beds spotlessly clean and uninhabited by other guests or any form of wildlife. Their predecessors, the early tourists of some 200 years ago, could not be so sure. Much of what they wrote of their experiences in this wild and remote corner of the country concerns the spectacular scenery which enthralled and occasionally horrified them, and it is only from scattered references that we are able to form an impression of the accommodation and hospitality they encountered. It was not only the 'stupendous crags' and the 'unhospitable terror' of the mountains that were part of the Lakeland experience for these adventurous gentlefolk.

Criticism of the plain and plentiful food they were offered is rare, even though some of the local dishes must have proved an unusual gastronomical experience; but rustic sleeping arrangements were often more irregular and austere than could be comfortably accepted.

In 1769 the poet Thomas Gray refused to stay at the Salutation Inn in Ambleside when he found 'the best bed-chamber' to be 'dark and damp as a cellar'. Sarah Aust, the Hon. Mrs Murray, staying at the King's Arms (now the Patterdale Hotel) in 1796, was 'obliged to pass the night in a chair by the kitchen fire, there not being a bed in the house fit to put myself upon'. Perhaps learning from this, she 'lodged a week very comfortably' at the Buttermere Inn 'with the help of my own sheets, blankets, pillows and counterpane'.[1]

It was at the inn in Patterdale that William Wordsworth, Walter Scott and Humphry Davy found their room already occupied by a party of ladies who sat talking until a very late hour, and appeared quite unperturbed by Scott and Davy loudly calling out the hours of the night beneath the window. On his visit to the inn at Rosthwaite, Wordsworth had to 'share a bed with a Scotch pedlar', an experience which shocked Robert Southey into declaring that 'he had rather not lie in bed the next forty years than sleep with a Scotch pedlar'. This was probably a less traumatic discovery, however, than that which greeted Mrs Eliza Lynn Linton, granddaughter of the Bishop of Carlisle, at the inn in Mardale where she found 'a tipsy parson in bed with his gin bottle by his side'.[2]

The 'many fleas' which inhabited John Keats' bed at the Nag's Head at Wythburn were, no doubt, less alarming but just as unwelcome. At least Matthew Arnold found the inn-keeper there a jovial fellow who 'shouted greetings from his easy chair' as his guests set off on their walk to Watendlath. It is reassuring too, to note that Joseph Budworth discovered the landlord at Patterdale to be 'a very well-informed man' and had only praise for Robert Newton's Inn in Grasmere. Samuel Taylor Coleridge considered the Traveller's Rest at Ulpha to be 'very nice' and 'the landlord a very intelligent man' – surely the same knowledgeable and quick-witted publican who, when presented by a group of noisy students with a request written in Latin, immediately replied in Greek which his guests were unable to translate.[3]

For the most part, however, the inn-keepers of the Lake District were quite unprepared to cater for these 'quality' visitors from the outside world. John Briggs was probably unlucky in his choice of the Kentmere Inn where the ale was 'nauseous' and where 'the floor was bespread with tubs, pans, tables, piggins,

The Salutation Hotel.

dishes, tins and other equipage of a farmer's kitchen' all of which had to be negotiated in order to get near the fire, and William Briggs, visiting the White Lion at Bowness in 1820 found a similar kitchen filled with guests through whom 'a greasy cook, who looked like one of her own puddings ready bagged for boiling', threaded her way, and 'among the rustics assembled round the fire . . . was the landlord whose face was the index to an excellent cellar.'[4]

Fortunately, the food and drink served in most Lakeland hostelries of the time met with general approval. Visitors took their meals at their inn and ate whatever the host provided. This would usually be plain country food such as might be served in almost any other part of the land but specifically local dishes would often be included.

The menu might feature Lakeland's most famous speciality, the char or Alpine trout, a delicacy served either fresh from the lakes or as potted char or even char-pie prepared in a large earthenware dish decorated with a picture of the fish itself. Dorothy

Wordsworth was much taken with the char from Seathwaite Tarn served for supper when she and William stayed at the Newfield Inn in the Duddon Valley, while Arthur Young enjoyed the renowned potted char of the King's Arms in Kendal, 'the best of any in the country' according to an earlier visitor, the much-travelled Celia Fiennes.[5]

There were certain country dishes which these sophisticated adventurers may well have regarded with some apprehension but which were part of the daily diet of the local population. One was 'crowdy', described as an excellent and invigorating species of soup made by pouring over oatmeal the liquid in which beef or mutton had been boiled. Oatmeal also figured prominently in 'poddish', a type of porridge made from oatmeal or barley boiled in water or milk, and eaten with bread and butter and sweetened with honey or treacle – a dish served to William and Dorothy Wordsworth when they stayed at the Star Inn in Martindale.

Poddish may have proved more palatable than a 'curious dish' described by Joseph Budworth without comment: 'Bread is cut into thin slices and placed in rows one above another in a large kettle … The butter and sugar are dissolved in a separate one, and then poured upon the bread, where it continues until it has boiled for some space, and the bread is perfectly saturated with the mixture; it is then taken out and served by way of dessert. This curious dish is called Buttered Sops.' This was probably an acquired taste as was the dried salted meat which Cumbrians apparently preferred to fresh meat until well into the nineteenth century. What Joseph Budworth actually thought of his buttered sops is not recorded, but both he and Arthur Young obviously relished the local apple puddings, the assortment of tarts and, especially, a dessert comprising 'three cups of preserved gooseberries with a bowl of rich cream in the centre'.[6]

Fine French wines in elegant glasses would not have graced

these inn tables but fine local ales, drunk from tankards, were always to be had, each household favouring its own distinctive brew. Budworth and the Hon. Mrs Murray were in agreement that the ale brewed at Buttermere was best of all: 'If you are fond of strong ales, I must tell you Buttermere is famous for it.' Very rarely an enterprising innkeeper would be able to provide his visitors with a noggin (a quarter of a pint) of rum or brandy. Buttermere was also awarded a five-star accolade by James Clarke for its fish – 'the best fish of any (Ullswater only excepted)' – and by Thomas Gray for its local mutton which 'nearly resembles venison'.[7]

Few tourists ventured to these chilly northern parts in spring but those who did would most probably be presented with herb pudding known in the Lake District as Easterledge pudding. Typical ingredients for this were large quantities of bistort and young nettles, a handful of chives, the leaves of blackcurrant, dandelion and bellflower, all chopped together with an onion and seasoned with salt and black pepper. Meat, usually veal, a beaten egg and a cupful of oatmeal and barley were added, and it was all boiled in a bag or baked in a dish. This healthy concoction would have seemed less strange in 1800 than it would today when recipes using many common herbs have been largely neglected or forgotten. Easterledge pudding may still be found in Cumbria today but it would be a brave chef who served it to the tourists.

The letters, journals and recollections compiled by the early tourists, although not so indecorous as to show a preoccupation with food and drink, do refer occasionally, and usually approvingly, to the meals provided by their Lakeland hosts. John Budworth, for example, staying in 1792 at Robert Newton's Inn at Grasmere (now Church Stile, the National Trust Information Centre) had 'as good and well-dressed a dinner ... as man could wish,' and at ten pence a head he considered it to be such good

The Inn at Buttermere, W. Green, 1809, 'if you are fond of strong ale, I must tell you, Buttermere is reckoned famous for it' (Joseph Budworth).

value that he wrote down the menu: 'Roast pike, stuffed; a boiled fowl; veal cutlets and ham; beans and bacon; cabbage, pease and potatoes; anchovy sauce; parsley and butter; plain butter; butter with cheese; wheat bread and oat cake; three cups of preserved gooseberries with a bowl of rich cream in the centre.' He added that he attempted to climb Helm Crag after dinner but found it 'formidable; and not less, to speak in plain English, from having a belly-full.' [8]

Budworth also regales us with details of the breakfast he enjoyed at the Cherry Tree Inn at Wythburn (a well-known hostelry which, like its rival half a mile away, the Nag's Head which boasted a sign painted by George Romney, was a casualty of the Thirlmere reservoir): 'They gave us breakfast fit for labouring men. We had mutton-ham, eggs, butter-milk, whey, tea, bread and butter, and they asked us if we chose to have any cheese, all for seven pence a piece.' [9]

It is a little surprising to see Budworth's reference to potatoes

David's Inn at Rydal, W. Green, 1809.

and tea for the former were almost unknown in Lakeland before the middle of the eighteenth century, and even then they were found only in a few locations, while tea although by that time becoming popular in some southern counties, was still little used in the north and was even regarded as an effeminate beverage – some eccentrics preferred to smoke it like tobacco. Perhaps a few enterprising innkeepers were quickly learning to cater for the more fashionable tastes of this new breed of visitor: although even in 1854 Harriet Martineau could complain that at the Red Lion in Grasmere 'the traveller's choice is usually between ham and eggs and eggs and ham.' [10]

Tourists who found accommodation in farmhouse or cottage appear to have been met with generous and spontaneous hospitality. Wordsworth and De Quincey, hungry after a long day's walking, called at High Bridge End farm in the Vale of St John and were 'ushered into a comfortable parlour' and warmly entertained by their physically intimidating host whose maid-servant told them that he 'would have brained us both if we had insulted him with the offer of money.' Eliza Lynn Linton received an equally hearty welcome when she called at a farmhouse in Heltondale, near Askham, seeking refreshment: she was offered 'wheaten bread, butter, and a huge jug of milk' and told to 'spare nothing' when presented with a large cheese specially for her from the 'rannel-balk'. [11]

The first tourists came to the Lake District primarily to view the scenery and to experience the thrill of close proximity to the 'horror' of 'vast precipices' and the 'frightful abyss'. They were also fascinated by 'curiosities' but found the entertainments on offer unsophisticated and undeniably rustic – the Low Wood Inn, near Ambleside, did boast 'an elegant upper room, furnished with a piano and an organ', but the guests at the Shap Wells Spa had to make do with 'a small jingling pianoforte and a bagatelle board' and 'dances where rank has no influence in the choice of partners', thus naively ignoring the rigid social distinctions of the

Robert Newton's Inn, Grasmere, R. Gambles, 2001.

time. At most inns the most likely amusement was the boisterous, bucolic romp known as a 'merry neet'. Wordsworth's poem *The Waggoner* gives a lively impression of the scene at The Cherry Tree Inn at Wythburn on one such occasion:

> 'Blythe souls and lightsome hearts have we
> Feasting at the Cherry Tree!
> What tankards foaming from the tap!
> What store of cakes in every lap!
> What thumping – stumping – overhead!'

Twenty miles away John Keats, staying at the Sun Inn at Ireby, gave his eye-witness account of a merry neet dance there: '...they kickit and jumpit with mettle extraordinary, and whiskit and friskit, and toe'd it and go'd it, twirled it and whirled it, and stamped it and sweated it tattooing the floor like mad. The difference between our country dances and these Scottish figures is about the same as leisurely stirring a cup of tea and beating a batter pudding.' [12]

All this was far removed from the sedate balls of the English country house and many of the early travellers to the mountain wilderness of the Lake District would probably be no more than amused spectators of these rustic hoe-downs, but would have treasured the experience as one of the memorable 'curiosities of our lake tour' together with the fleas, the poddish and the 'nauseous ale' of Kentmere. They did, at least, savour something of the local culture as well as gaze in awe at the beauty and horror of the mountain landscape.

6

A Chain of Amusements

IN 1990 the panel set up to review the aims and purposes of the National Parks made a strong recommendation that 'the forms of outdoor recreations to be encouraged in national parks should only be those which involve the quiet enjoyment of the areas'.[1] This was an attempt to stem the tide of inappropriate tourist activities which threaten the tranquillity of the national parks, a judgement which echoed the observation on the Lake District by William Gilpin two hundred years earlier that 'every part is filled with those engaging passages of nature which tend to sooth the mind and instil tranquillity'.[2]

In the late eighteenth century as the influx of tourists into the Lake District began to swell from a modest trickle to a steady (if seasonal) stream there were already those who were quick to realise that there was money to be made from tourism and were busy developing the first tourist attractions. Climbing and fell-walking were not yet popular pursuits, and there was, after all, a limit to the number of 'picturesque scenes' one could view through a Claude glass each day with sustained enthusiasm, and lifting one's eyes to the hills in search of spiritual enlightenment or 'thoughts that do often lie too deep for tears' can be mentally exhausting. There was clearly an opportunity to provide diversions and entertainments and especially of the kind which would appeal to the increasing number of the *nouveaux riches* from the northern industrial towns as well as to the gentry from London familiar with the music, fireworks and other amusements at the Vauxhall Gardens.

Among the first of these entrepreneurs was Peter Crosthwaite, an astute if ill-tempered Keswick eccentric, who quickly sensed the 'needs' of tourists and how he could provide for them. He saw that Thomas West's 'stations' could often be difficult for visitors to locate and so he produced a remarkably accurate series of maps furnished with details of the viewpoints, local roads, depths of the lakes and other features of interest. These proved to be so popular that Crosthwaite took pains to update them as each edition sold out.

Low Wood Inn, Windermere – T. Fielding, 1842

He claimed to have sold 'many thousand' of his maps to tourists who visited his famous museum, a bizarre collection of assorted curiosities. To attract attention to his museum Crosthwaite had an arrangement of drums, a barrel organ and a Chinese gong to create a thunderous noise whenever a carriage bearing likely customers appeared in the vicinity, an advertising ruse which seems to have been successful. In 1793, according to

Crosthwaite's calculations, 1,540 'persons of rank and fashion' paid their shilling admission fee (sixpence for those not classified as 'ladies and gentlemen'), thereby qualifying to have their names printed in a weekly list of visitors which Crosthwaite placed in the *Cumberland Pacquet*.

Among the motley collection which greeted them, apart from the more orthodox museum items such as fossils, stuffed birds and minerals, were two barnacles from Captain Cook's ship, the hand of an Egyptian mummy, a straw hat worn by a sailor who had been with Captain Bligh on the *Bounty*, a chicken with two heads and a lamb with wool of three colours, the rib-bone of a giant, and a 'geological piano'. This was a set of sixteen musical stones, cut and shaped by Crosthwaite himself, and tuned to cover two octaves, an invention which inspired others in Keswick to create more elaborate and sophisticated musical stone instruments which toured the country and even performed before Queen Victoria. Visitors to the museum could also purchase Claude glasses, guidebooks, engravings and, of course, Crosthwaite's maps. Not everyone found this 'Cabinet of Curiosities' an enthralling experience: William Gell, topographer and guidebook writer, bluntly commented in 1797, 'His daughter is an elegant woman and more worth seeing than anything else in his house'.[3]

Equally as eccentric as Crosthwaite, but with much more grandiose schemes to attract tourists, was Joseph Pocklington, a successful business man from Nottingham, who purchased Vicar's Island in Derwentwater, renamed it Pocklington's Island, and proceeded to transform it, first by constructing a mansion aptly described by Norman Nicholson as 'laughably ugly'. This was followed by an ornate fort bristling with brass cannon, a boat-house which looked like a chapel, a church which looked like a doll's house, and a model of Castlerigg Stone Circle, all set against a 'ghost' tree, a mutilated oak tree, the bark shaved off

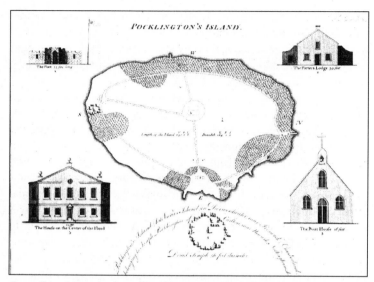

Peter Crosthwaite's plan of Pocklington's Island. The island was known as Vicar's Island until 1778 and was given its modern name, Derwent Island, by Pocklington's successor in 1797.

the trunk, and the skeleton covered in whitewash.

Pocklington next embarked on an enterprising plan to introduce what Wordsworth dismissed as 'a new fashion' and James Clarke described as 'a species of entertainment'. At Ousebridge, on Bassenthwaite Lake, Pocklington arranged an event of aquatic diversions which attracted large crowds. A number of horses were rowed out on a raft to the centre of the lake and then turned off into the water. Bets were laid and the first horse to swim ashore was declared the winner. Another 'excellent diversion' was the release of a duck into the water to be chased by several water spaniels spurred on by crowds on the shore.[4]

The success of the cavortings on Bassenthwaite inspired Pocklington to plan a far more ambitious 'entertainment' on Derwentwater. On 28 August 1781 the first Keswick Regatta was held with Pocklington himself as 'Governor and Commander-in-Chief of the Island' and Peter Crosthwaite as 'Admiral and Commander-in-Chief of the Fleet'. Proceedings began with a discharge of artillery from the island fort. Competitors in the boat races were cheered on by large crowds assembled at various vantage points or accommodated in marquees erected on the shoreline or on pleasure barges 'tricked out in all the gayest colours'. James Clarke was fortunate enough to find a reliable eye-witness account of the day's events:

> About three o'clock preparations were made for the sham attack on Pocklington's Island. The fleet, consisting of several barges, armed with small cannon and musquets, retired out of view behind Friar-Cragg, to prepare for action; previous to which a flag of truce was sent to the Governor, with a summons to surrender upon honourable

Bassenthwaite Lake, T. Allom, 1833. "Poor Bassenthwaite scarcely gets its due." Eliza Lynn Linton indicates that this lake was little visited by the early tourists.

terms. A defiance was returned; soon after which the fleet was seen advancing with great spirit before the batteries, and instantly forming in a curved line, a terrible cannonading began on both sides accompanied with a dreadful discharge of musquetry.

This continued for some time, and being echoed from hill to hill in an amazing variety of sounds, filled the ear with whatever could produce astonishment and awe. All nature seemed to be in an uproar … After a severe conflict, the enemies were driven from the attack in great disorder. A *feu de joye* was then fired in the fort, and oft repeated by the responsive echoes. The fleet … formed again … and renewed the attack. Uproar again sprung up, and the deep-toned echoes of the mountains again joined in solemn chorus; which was heard, to the distance of ten leagues … as far as Appleby.

The garrison at last capitulated; and the entertainment of the water being finished, (towards the evening), the company moved to Keswick; to which place, from the water's edge, a range of lamps was fixed, very happily disposed, and a number of fireworks displayed off. An Assembly-room (which was built for the purpose) next received the Ladies and Gentlemen, and a dance concluded this annual festivity.* A chain of amusements, which we may venture to offer no other place can possibly furnish, and which wants only to be more universally known, to render it a place of more general resort than any in the kingdom'.[5]

Three years later the level of noise at the Regatta was raised by the addition of the sound of French horns which alternated with the firing of the guns, creating, according to Clarke, 'pleasing sounds, which when softened and reverberated by innumerable cliffs exhibit an almost supernatural harmony.' This form of tourist entertainment was soon taken up by the Duke of Norfolk who hired out barges to take tourists across Ullswater to a designated picnic spot and, as William Hutchinson described the scene:

---

* *except for 'The Nobility and Gentry' who, the programme announced, were invited to dine in Keswick 'where all things necessary will be provided.'*

While we sat to regale, the barge put off from the shore to a station where the finest echoes were to be obtained from the surrounding mountains. The vessel was provided with six brass cannon mounted on swivels; on discharging one of these pieces the report echoed from the opposite rocks … The report of every discharge was re-echoed seven times distinctly 'in a kind of wondrous tumult and grandeur' to be followed at intervals by 'the music of two French horns whose harmony was repeated from every recess which echo haunted on the borders of the lake.[6]

Not to be outshone by either Joseph Pocklington or the Duke of Norfolk, John Curwen of Belle Isle assembled a fleet of seventeen colourful vessels rowed by oarsmen clad in brilliant scarlet uniforms to provide similar entertainment for tourists at Windermere. The Windermere Regatta was a sedate affair consisting mainly of sailing races but there were also more plebeian sports such as wrestling, 'leaping' and footraces. By 1790 enthusiasm for the Keswick Regatta had begun to fade and it had a distinctly chequered future whereas the Windermere Regatta went from strength to strength receiving a fulsome entry in Parson and White's *Directory* of 1829:

The lake on these festive days is crowded with boats and elegant barges, forming splendid aquatic processions attended by bands of music and filled with gay and mirthful parties … with rowing, sailing and wrestling matches … balls at inns, exhibitions of fireworks, etc.

Meanwhile Pocklington was adding to his 'chain of amusements'. The Bowder Stone, widely believed to be 'the largest stone in England', was already a popular tourist attraction but Pocklington felt its entertainment value could be improved. A hole was excavated beneath the huge boulder through which visitors prepared to lie prone under nearly 2,000 tons of rock could shake hands. For those who wished to climb to the top of the stone a ladder

KESWICK REGATTA.

THE
REGATTA
AND
GREAT ENGAGEMENT,
ON THE
CELEBRATED LAKE OF DERWENT,
WILL BE ON

FRIDAY the *Twenty-Eighth* of AUGUST, 1789.

A Prize of Six Guineas will be given to the winning Boat. If more than Three Boats start, the Second shall be entitled to Three Guineas, and the Third to Two Guineas. No Person will be allowed to row, who has rowed at any former *Regatta* at Keswick.

Regatta BOATS to be conformable to such Regulations as the Steward or his Deputy shall think proper.

FORT JOSEPH, near the Block House, on Pocklington's Island, will be attacked immediately on the finishing of the Boat Race; and Signals, during the Attack, will be made from the Battery upon EUROPA POINT, with heavy Metal, which will be repeated by the Mountains.

There will also be several other curious Pieces of Entertainment.

The Boats to start at Half past Eleven o'Clock, and all Diversions, except the BALL, to be finished at Three o'Clock in the Afternoon.

☞ The NOBILITY and GENTRY to dine in the Long Room in Keswick, immediately after ; where all Things necessary will be provided:

And in Order to the Engagement being conducted handsomely, it is particularly desired by the great Officers, That no Boats will come near the Grand Fleet during the Time of the Engagement, nor any Person enter either into the Fleet or Army, but such as will readily obey Orders, and pay a due Regard to Signals.

Individuals not to enrich themselves with Plunder, but *share and share alike.*— And be it well remembered, that too much Live-Lumber, upon the Deck of any Vessel, hinders the Working of the Guns, and endangers the whole Crew.

WILFRID LAWSON, Esq.
Steward.

JOSEPH POCKLINGTON, Esq.
Governor and Commander in Chief of the Island.

PETER CROSTHWAITE,
Admiral and Commander in Chief of the Fleet.

[*J. WARE & SON, PRINTERS, WHITEHAVEN.*]

some 36 feet long was provided – the reward for the scary ascent was a fine prospect into Borrowdale viewed over a 'Druid monolith' set up nearby by the ever-resourceful Pocklington.[7]

Windermere Regatta – T. Unwins.

Crosthwaite and Pocklington had undoubtedly made Keswick the mecca of popular tourism by the 1790s – Ambleside, however, remained the resort for the more elite visitor to the Lake District – but before long there were voices raised in protest against these noisy and incongruous intrusions on the tranquil Lakeland scene. The formidable Honourable Mrs Sarah Murray left no doubt of her opinion in her 'Companion and useful Guide' of 1797:

Were I a nymph of Derwentwater I should, like Niobe, weep myself to a statue for the injury committed on taste and nature by the erections of that gentleman on one of the islands and on the banks of this charming lake; for, Mr Pocklington's slime may be traced in every part of Keswick Vale. It is a pity he has no friend to advise him to blow to atoms everything he has constructed and planned.[8]

For the time being this was a voice crying in the wilderness. By the early years of the new century a 'tourist trail' had been established in and around Keswick. Within the town itself there were two rival museums, concerts in the Town Hall, a pavilion to accommodate 2,000 people for equestrian events, a library, and a rather rudimentary theatre where Joseph Budworth 'went to see *The Merchant of Venice* in an unroofed house' which he found so uncomfortable that he left commenting that 'some of the actors performed very well, others rather middling'.[9]

The Bowder Stone, J. Harwood, 1842. Harwood's engraving shows Pocklington's cottage erected for the old woman 'curator', his 'druidicial' megalith, and the ladder for visitors to climb to the top of the boulder to admire the view into Borrowdale.

The lake itself was a major attraction with large numbers of rowing boats often hired for the popular pastime of fishing. The success of Pocklington's gunfire echoes was also taken up by others on Derwentwater including the Duke of Portland who equipped a ten-seater barge with a cannon which reverberated loudly in the surrounding hills. The Lodore Falls when in spate was an exciting spectacle but to avoid disappointment when it was no more than a trickle the proprietor of the inn who kept the key had installed two cannon which could produce greater or lesser echoes: to fire the larger gun one paid four shillings and for the smaller amount of two shillings and sixpence, fees which Robert Southey declared 'made English echoes ... the most expensive luxuries in which a traveller can indulge.'[10] In the hills above the Falls of Lodore lies the tiny hamlet of Watendlath then, as now, a magnet for tourists with its ancient farmsteads and cottages nestling by a lovely tarn and a neat little packhorse bridge: William Gilpin, like so many others, enthused that it was 'a place of scenery which for beauty, and grandeur, was equal, if not superior, to anything we had yet seen'.[11]

Also on the tourist trail was a much less exhilarating spot in

Watendlath and the stream of Lowdore, T. Allom, 1833 "a piece of scenery which for beauty and grandeur was equal, if not superior, to anything we had yet seen," W. Gilpin.

the boggy flatlands between Derwentwater and Lake Bassenthwaite. The Manesty salt spring, well-known to the monks of Furness Abbey, was enjoying a new popularity as the eighteenth century cult for spa water developed as a cure for almost every ailment known to mankind. By the mid-nineteenth century tourists, some with genuine illness, some with imagined complaints, others just curious, were flocking to the many Lakeland spas which were established to exploit this latest medical affectation. Gilsland, Stanger, Humphrey Head and Shap Wells had a steady clientele, (see Chapter 10). Manesty's salt waters were already known in 1740 to confer the benefit of 'a rough, severe purge to strong constitutions' and to be effective in the treatment of a catalogue of ailments which most people were unaware of. Most tourists visited the Manesty salt spring out of curiosity not for a health cure.

More exciting, perhaps, but much more unpredictable, was an excursion to Derwentwater's floating island. This natural phenomenon appeared on twenty occasions between 1770 and 1830 and was referred to in almost every guidebook. Its size, shape and solidity varied greatly: it would sometimes have a safe, if somewhat soggy, weight-bearing capacity. Joseph Budworth noted that 'there are very few people in the neighbourhood who have not been upon it.' This unprepossessing mass of peat, rotting vegetation and aquatic plants which mysteriously rose to the surface of the lake for a few days or weeks and then disappeared again was a 'must' for the early tourists, but by the 1880s scientific investigation had destroyed its mystery – methane gas was not part of the tourist agenda – and the guide books rarely referred to it. Baddeley's Guide in late Victorian times dismissed it as 'hardly worth mentioning'. Its last appearance in the hot summer of 2003 passed almost unnoticed.[12]

A short distance from Keswick stands the most magnificently

The floating island of Derwentwater, W. Westall, 1820s. This natural phenomenon now appears very rarely but between 1770 and 1830 it rose to the surface twenty times and fascinated tourists.

sited prehistoric stone circle in the country. 'Of all the superb rings in the Lake District,' wrote Aubrey Burl in 1979, 'the Castlerigg Stone Circle is the most exciting and the most mysterious,' and it has been described as 'one of the most visually impressive prehistoric monuments in Britain.' To most eighteenth and nineteenth century visitors it was a 'Druid's Circle' and guides stimulated their imaginations with improbable but widely believed tales of Druidical rituals. The stones, in fact, predate the Druids by at least one or two thousand years and were most probably a neolithic assembly point for religious or secular purposes or, as recent theorists would claim, for astronomical observations. Whatever the true purpose of the Castlerigg Circle may have been few eighteenth century tourists could resist an urge to share Thomas Gray's experience there:

Castlerigg stone circle, T. Allom, 1830s.

A Druid circle of large stones, one hundred and eight feet in diameter, the biggest not eight feet high, but most of them still erect: they are fifty in number ... the sun breaking out, discovered the most enchanting view I have yet seen of the whole valley behind me, the two lakes, the river, the mountains in all their glory.[13]

A century later Castlerigg was attracting a different breed of tourist for in late Victorian times: it was reported that 'huge chara-bancs daily discharge large numbers of tourists and trippers at the circle, who proceed to cut their initials on the stones.'[14]

The axis of early tourism lay emphatically on a well-defined route between Windermere and Keswick with excursions to Buttermere, Lorton and Newlands (the Buttermere Round), and to Ullswater. Few visitors ventured into remote areas such as Eskdale or Wasdale. The search for the 'picturesque' and the 'romantic' could be conducted in comparative comfort in private or hired coaches driven along roads recently given a surface less calculated to break wheels or displace vertebrae than those which existed a generation before. Within an acceptable distance were almost all the notable 'stations' specified by West's *Guide*, the historical sites and 'curiosities' noted by Hutchinson, and the beauty spots and places of romantic legend made famous by the Lake Poets.

7

THAT'S WHERE WE SPILT THE POET

NORMAN Nicholson's observation that after 1790 tourists in Lakeland 'were no longer pioneers or explorers; they were holiday-makers,'[1] implied that a visit to the Lake District was no longer looked upon as an adventure into the wilderness. A succession of guidebooks had changed a tour of Lakeland from a voyage of discovery into a planned itinerary designed to visit specified beauty spots, curiosities, sites of historic interest, dubious legends and droll or singular folk-tales. Visitors, guidebook in hand or hired guide by their side, were directed where to go, what to see, how to appreciate what they saw and regaled with instructive or entertaining tit-bits of information on the way. Wordsworth attempted to point the way to a deeper appreciation of the district in his famous *Guide to the Lakes* but by the 1840s guidebooks such as Black's *Picturesque Guide* and *Bradshaw and Blacklock's Guide* were setting the pattern for the modern travel book with comprehensive practical detail on every aspect of a tourist's needs in his chosen destination: how to get there, where to stay, the hire of guides and ponies for mountain expeditions, directions for local walks, the timetables and cost of excursions by coach, wagonette or lake steamer, and detailed guidance to every place of tourist interest.[2]

There were a few local residents such as William and Dorothy Wordsworth, Samuel Taylor Coleridge, Elizabeth Smith and her sister, and Thomas Wilkinson who ventured to 'scale the icy mountains' lofty tops' and wrote appreciatively of the experience, but most visitors were fearful of the high fells and embarked on an expedition to the summits only with a guide in attendance, and their accounts often did little to encourage others to follow in their footsteps. Thus even Joseph Budworth, a pioneer among tourist fell-walkers, on descending Pike of Stickle, relates that his guide 'tied up my right eye, which could not have borne the vast precipice almost perpendicularly under me'; Sir Edward Baines found Helvellyn, and particularly Striding Edge, quite terrifying: 'if we had had a guide, all this would have been much less terrific because he would have led the way, and shown us where to place every footstep'; Ellen Weeton, the feisty governess from Dove Nest, was delighted with all that she saw from the summit of Fairfield but when she found herself 'seated upon its projecting point and a direct perpendicular descent on every side but one … such a degree of terror overpowered me that I durst no longer behold it … I remained a considerable time before I dared rise and make a retreat.'

As late as the 1840s Black's *Picturesque Guide to the English Lakes* issued dire warnings to those thinking of undertaking the exhilarating walk from Wasdale Head to Buttermere via Black Sail Pass and Scarth Gap: 'the hardy pedestrian with very minute direc-

Aira Force, T. Allom, 1830s.

tions might succeed in finding his way over the mountains, yet everyone who has crossed them will be aware of the danger of the attempt, and of the occasional fatal consequences attending a diversion from the proper path.' This was a section of a tourist 'round-trip' excursion by coach and on foot from Keswick to Wasdale Head via Styhead and return to a hearty meal at the Buttermere Inn where a coach waited to transport the party back to Keswick; one might not guess from the guidebook's unnerving account that this was a well-trodden path familiar to generations of local shepherds and scores of pannier-laden packhorses.[3]

Skiddaw, by contrast, was promoted as the ultimate tourist attraction. It was (and is) the least demanding of the high fells to climb; it was (wrongly) believed to be the highest mountain in England; and its virtues had been extolled in prose and poetry for over a hundred years. Wordsworth considered it to be superior to Mount Parnassus itself; Ellen Weeton expressed her opinion that 'The great and noble Skiddaw is among mountains what Dr Johnson was amongst authors,' while for Charles Lamb its ascent was 'a day that will stand out, like a mountain, I am sure, all my life.'[4]

Stock Gill Force, Ambleside, T. Allom, 1830s.

Wordsworth and a party of family, friends, a number of tourists and a few locals assembled round a huge bonfire on Skiddaw summit on 21 August 1815, to celebrate the victory at Waterloo. Robert Southey described the occasion:

> We roasted beef and boiled plum puddings there; sung *God save the King* round the most furious body of flaming tar barrels that I ever saw; drank a huge wooden bowl of punch; fired a cannon at every health with three times three, and rolled large balls of tow and turpentine down the steep side of the mountain. The effect was grand beyond imagination ...

Wordsworth accidentally knocked over the kettle holding the hot water used to dilute the rum punch and this greatly enlivened the subsequent festivities as most of the party became reconciled to drinking their celebratory beverage undiluted. The descent at the end of the evening must have been a startling sight for the sober citizens of Keswick: Southey relates that:

> All our torches were lit at once by this mad company, and our way down the hill was marked by a track of fire from flambeaux dropping pitch, tarred ropes, etc. One fellow was so drunk that his companions placed him on a horse, with his face to the tail to bring him down, themselves being just sober enough to guide and hold him on.[5]

In the 1830s a young John Ruskin described a more typical tourist excursion to Skiddaw portraying a scene more reminiscent of a departure for a European tour. Guides, ponies and tourists fuss busily as the elaborate preparations proceed: vast quantities of food have to be safely packed, together with several flasks of brandy and other drinks; spare riding skirts for all the ladies have to be checked, ribbons secured to tie-on hats, cloaks and loose mantles provided against possible wind and rain and chilly air on the summit. Mary Lamb, we learn from her brother's account, 'was excessively tired when she got about half-way up Skiddaw' but was revived by 'a draught of cold water' and reached the summit 'most manfully'. Most ladies experienced little difficulty on Skiddaw for, as Elizabeth Lynn Linton commented, 'the most timid horse-woman can ride to the top without a really hard pinch anywhere', but Sir Edward Baines was taking no risks when he climbed Helvellyn in 1829 – the ladies were left behind as the journey was too perilous.[6]

Colwith Force, Little Langdale.

Two centuries later we may perhaps raise a superior smile at the fear of the high fells felt by so many of the first tourists and their assumption that it was prudent to hire a guide for almost any expedition above the valley floor. Today, and for the past hundred years, fell-walkers have had at their disposal a variety of detailed maps and guidebooks covering every route to the fell-tops and offering advice on mountain safety and suitable clothing and footwear. None of this existed for the pioneers of fell-walking and the dangers they could encounter without a guide are well illustrated by the adventures of Samuel Taylor Coleridge on his walking tour in 1802: having successfully climbed Scafell he then decided to conquer Scafell Pike but, map-less and guide-less, he was unaware that there is no direct route for walkers from one peak to the other, and proceeded to descend the precipitous crag of Broad Stand being forced to drop from narrow ledge to narrow ledge, a trap from which he was very lucky to escape with his life.[7] It is also worth noting that it was in the summer of 1805 that the tale of Charles Gough, who fell to his death off Striding Edge and was not discovered until three months later, was on everyone's lips – a grim warning to timid tourists, most of whom were content to enjoy visits and guided tours to sites and scenes at less exalted heights.

Waterfalls were a popular tourist attraction and most guidebooks of the time drew attention to those which were readily accessible. The cascades of Sour Milk Gill and Moss Force could be admired from the road at Buttermere Church or Newlands Hause. Stockghyll Force, Aira Force and Rydal Falls were the rewards for a pleasant and undemanding walk; and all three were endowed with a fairy-tale glamour by the poetic musings of Keats and Wordsworth and (for Aira Force) a tale of medieval love and tragedy of the type which appealed so strongly to the Victorian age.

Scale Force – T. Allom, 1830s.

75

Skiddaw

The legend was recounted in Wordsworth's poem *The Som-nambulist*: Sir Eglamore, a knight-errant, and Lady Emma whose home was by the lake not far from the falls, were deeply in love, but Sir Eglamore had to fulfil his 'quest' and while he was away Emma, distraught at his long absence, began to walk in her sleep. On his return her knight found her asleep on the edge of Aira Force. He touched her gently to wake her, but she was so startled that she lost her balance, fell into the torrent and drowned.[8]

Scale Force, Lakeland's highest waterfall, was inevitably on every tourist's list, but to reach it involved a walk of about a mile over rough and boggy terrain. A boat was hired to cross Crum-mock Water to Ling Crag where the path to the force began; a causeway was laid across the wettest places to make access easier but this has now almost disappeared. Joseph Budworth, having casually doubled the actual height of Scale Force, enthusiastically extolled it as 'a musical abyss', 'one of the most inimitable scenes that ever enriched the fancy of man'. Elizabeth Lynn Linton was somewhat less romantic in her account: 'It is pleasant among these slippery rocks, where, if you do plunge knee-deep in the pools, you come to no vital harm.'[9]

The showpiece among waterfalls was in the grounds of Rydal Hall. The Rydal Cascades were visited, painted and eulogised by innumerable artists, poets and writers. A special feature here was the grotto, a summer house or 'viewing house', with a window facing directly to the cascades to present a perfectly framed picture, a device which precisely met William Gilpin's idea of the 'picturesque', even though it was constructed a hundred years earlier, in 1669. Even William Gell, not one given to flourishes of enthusiasm in his interpretation of the scenery, was impelled

to bestow a rare accolade on the grotto: 'a little summer house which ... presented us through a large square window with a miniature of as beautiful and romantic a fall of water as the imagination can conceive'; and John Stuart Mill who had declared crabbily that a waterfall in itself gave him little pleasure, produced the felicitous image of the falls as 'the most brilliant passages in a fine piece of music'. When Queen Adelaide came to visit Wordsworth at Rydal

Lower Falls at Rydal, G. Pickering, 1830s

77

*Upper Falls at Rydal,
H. Gastineau, 1830s.*

Mount he escorted her without delay to see the Rydal Cascades, so highly did he regard them and so famous a landmark had they become by 1840.[10]

Another favourite walk for the Wordsworths and for many of the more energetic tourists was to Easedale and the cascades of Sourmilk Gill (or Churnmilk Force as it was then known). Here, as one approaches up the rough track, the waters appear to emerge from no apparent source before they pour foaming over the tumbled rocks and huge boulders which lie in their path. Many of those who made this expedition were tempted to walk an extra half-mile to Easedale Tarn, a true mountain tarn in a romantic setting surrounded by grassy moraines and formidable crags. Moreover, an enterprising Victorian had established close by the waters of the tarn that magnet for tired and footsore English tourists, a tearoom, now no more than a scatter of stones.

The vagaries of the weather in the Lake District often mean that the waterfalls are less than impressive. A succession of fine days can reduce the flow of water dramatically and this is nowhere better demonstrated than in the popular and much lauded Falls of Lodore in Borrowdale. Peter Crosthwaite's map of 1809 referred to them as 'The great Waterfall' and Thomas West's *Guide* of 1778 called them 'the Niagara of the Lake', while Robert Southey gave them everlasting fame with his long 'Lodore-shaped' poem, 'How does the Water Come down at Lodore'. The cleft through which the falls descend is impressive in itself, a wooded chasm between Shepherd's Crag and Gowder Crag, and after heavy rain the falls are indeed an unforgettable sight – West's reference to Niagara was not quite as

Lowdore cataract by Thomas Allom

fanciful as it might seem; the actual difference in the 'drop' of water is less than four metres. Niagara, however, is never lacking in water, but many a visitor to Lodore has been disappointed to see only a pile of damp and mossy boulders. A tale told by guides referred to a forlorn tourist who asked where he could find the famous Falls of Lodore only to receive the reply:

'Sir, you are sitting in them'.

A repertoire of such tales – apocryphal or not – was part of the store of information carried by guides, coach-drivers, innkeepers and boatmen. 'The watermen and guides,' wrote James Clarke, 'think they must tell the tourists some extraordinary tale or other, and therefore endeavour to invent something that bears the face of probability'. Two tales from Borrowdale confirmed for urban visitors the widespread belief that the folk of this valley were unusually backward and unintelligent. The first related how the inhabitants were always so relieved when spring-time and the sound of the cuckoo returned that they planned to keep spring all the year by building a wall round the valley to prevent the cuckoo from flying away. Inevitably, the plot failed and as the cuckoo sailed

Lady's Rake, Borrowdale.

over the wall one dalesman declared that if only they had added another line of stones to the wall the bird would never have got away.

Colour photographs by Val Corbett on following pages:

Aira Force with rainbow spray.
Ullswater from Place Fell.
Swan on Rydal Water.
Blea Tarn with the Langdale Pikes.
A Host of Golden Daffodils.
Blelham Tarn and Windermere towards Fairfield.
Grasmere
Geese on Derwentwater towards Cat Bells.

The other tale might easily have contained a grain of truth: this concerned a local lad sent to collect a load of lime and he panicked when it began to smoke in a sudden shower of rain. He ran to fetch water from the nearby river to throw over his cargo thus making the situation so much worse. Perhaps the most popular tale from Borrowdale was that of Lady's Rake, the steep gully in the middle of Walla Crag. This was traditionally pointed out as the route taken by Lady Derwentwater when she escaped her pursuers after her husband had been arrested for his involvement in the Jacobite Rebellion of 1715. On her way she dropped her handkerchief which could clearly be seen more than a century later - an occasional coating of limewash on a prominent rock was all that was required to lend credence to the story.

We have already noted the appeal of tales of human misfortune in the sad fate of Emma at Aira Force. Tourists would hear similar stories elsewhere, some pure invention, some based on real events. Among the latter was the tragic misadventure in 1808 of George and Sarah Green who lived with their seven children at Blindtarn Gill in Easedale. The parents had walked over the felltops to Langdale to attend a sale but as they returned they lost their way in terrible weather conditions. When they failed to arrive back home two days later, Sally the oldest child, went to a neighbour to raise the alarm. Sixty dales folk began a search and discovered the bodies of George and Sarah at the foot of the precipice known as Eagle Crag. The seven orphans were taken care of by local people and a fund of £600 (an enormous sum at that time) was raised to support them. Dorothy Wordsworth wrote a moving account of their story which had the additional poignancy of a contemporary tragedy.[11]

Travellers along Leathes Water (Thirlmere) paused by a rocky promontory, (now under the waters of the reservoir), to hear the remarkable tale of a man who had decided to put an end to his life, precisely why is far from clear, but in his decision he apparently had the full support of his wife. They discussed together the best way to achieve his objective. She dissuaded him from poisoning, hanging or shooting himself as these methods could be painful and uncertain, but suggested drowning as a preferable alternative. When he proposed wading straight into the lake, she said he would suffer needless discomfort from the cold water; it would be far better to find a suitable crag to plunge directly into deep water. Eventually they found a spot and she advised him to take a run and a leap to make sure that he did not strike the rocks below. This he duly did and his wife stayed until she was sure that he was safely drowned. The spot was subsequently known as Clark's Leap.

James Clarke, in his *Survey of the Lakes*, relates that he sought out the woman in 1789 with 'the curiosity ... to ask it from her own mouth'; she was, he said, 'fully satisfied that she had done her duty in giving him the best advice she could'.[12] At almost the same time a story was unfolding a few miles away which had all

The Fish Inn at Buttermere.

the ingredients of a romantic novel.

During his tour through the Lake District in the 1790s Joseph Budworth had been captivated by the beauty of the daughter of the landlord of the Fish Inn at Buttermere and wrote such a rhapsody of her charms that before long tourists were beating a path to her door. Among them was a lone traveller claiming to be The Honourable Colonel Alexander Augustus Hope, MP,

Mary Robinson and John Hatfield, from Cassell's magazine.

brother of the Earl of Hopetoun, who immediately set out to seduce Mary and inveigle her into marriage. In this he was eventually successful, but Budworth had given Mary such national fame that her wedding was reported in the London press and read by acquaintances of the real Colonel Hope, who knew that he was not in Buttermere at that time.

The imposter was exposed as a bigamist, seducer, fraudster and bankrupt who had abandoned his wife and daughters as he now abandoned his new bride to her shame and distress. He was arrested and sent for trial at Carlisle Assizes under his real name, John Hatfield. He was executed for his crimes in September 1803. Mary subsequently made a happy marriage to a local farmer. Her death in 1837 was reported in the London Annual Register which described her as the far-famed and much talked of Mary of Buttermere, the 'Buttermere Beauty'. Her story attracted tourists to

Thirlmere's bridges by T. Allom, 1835. At this time Thirlmere was formed of two lakes, Leathes Water and Wythburn Water, with a causeway and bridges at the narrowest point.

the Fish Inn throughout the nineteenth century and became the theme of many plays, poems and novels, most recently in Melvyn Bragg's novel, *Maid of Buttermere.*

A tale more likely to raise a laugh was the discomfiting of the Bishop of Carlisle when he imprudently intervened to halt a local lying contest, delivering 'a severe lecture on the iniquity of such a proceeding and ending with the pompous assertion: 'For my part I never told a lie in my life.' The judges unanimously agreed that this deserved to be awarded the winner's prize.[13]

Tourists of the Georgian and early Victorian age were as notable in their enthusiasm for visiting stately homes and for getting close to 'celebrities' as their successors today. There were few country mansions in Lakeland, but there were a number of famous literary figures who made a permanent or temporary home there, the most celebrated of whom was William Wordsworth whose visitors' book at Rydal Mount contained 2,500 names. An

William Wordsworth.

anonymous journal of 1849 records the following revealing entry:

> There was much debating as to the boldness required to get an en-
> trance into Wordsworth's grounds … We got permission to go in
> and took a long time to our walk in hopes of seeing him … we found
> old Miss Wordsworth in a wheelchair and as she is out of her mind
> … we came away, and our consideration was rewarded by seeing
> Wordsworth slowly ascending the hill as we went to our carriage.
> We of course walked very slowly and had a very good view of
> him.[14]

Wordsworth appears to have viewed all this attention with equanimity or indifference, but he was less philosophical about an incident which occurred some years earlier. He was driving in his chaise along the road to Keswick near Shoulthwaite when the heavy Whitehaven to London mail-coach approached at speed and failed to avoid a collision. The coach-driver himself added the tale to his repertoire: 'Crash went the shay (chaise) all to smithereens right through a drystone wall and slap went the driver over into a plantation, arms out and greatcoat flying. And now, gentlemen, when you next go to Keswick, just by the bridge about three miles out, you'll see two yards of the wall down to this day, and that's where we spilt the poet.' Wordsworth appears not to have been inspired to commemorate this disaster in verse.[15]

Less than a mile away, across the valley, looms the massive crag known as Castle Rock, which achieved fame and a fanciful new name in 1805 when Walter Scott, inspired by an unusually colourful passage in Hutchinson's *Excursion to the Lakes*, wrote

Rydal Mount, a sketch by Dora Wordsworth 1841, home of William Wordsworth.

Castle Rock, Vale of St. John, photograph by the author.

his narrative poem *The Bridal of Triermain,* a tale of medieval romance and chivalry with many of the Arthurian characters beloved by the Victorians. Castle Rock became a fortified medieval stronghold within which were imprisoned the fair Gwyneth and her treacherous mother Gwendolen. King Arthur and Sir Roland de Vaux came to rescue their ladies while Sir Gawain fought his duel with the Green Knight nearby. For those who wished to believe, Scott's romantic and dramatic description of this 'banner'd castle, keep and tower' and of the final assault on its ramparts, served to place the Castle Rock of Triermain firmly on the tourist trail.

King Arthur was also invoked at two ancient historical sites near Penrith: Mayburgh Henge and King Arthur's Round Table, henge monuments which probably had more visitors then than they have today. The cult of the Arthurian legend was widely followed at that time and there were eager listeners to the story of how Sir Lancelot du Lac freed 64 of Arthur's knights here from the giant Tarquin and how 50 knights jousted here to win the hand of Arthur's daughter, Gwyneth. 'We were induced to believe,' wrote Hutchinson, 'that this was an ancient tilting ground.'

Other prehistoric circles were widely believed (wrongly) to be Druidical in origin and so well furnished with gruesome accounts of human and animal sacrifices, pagan rituals and strange and dubious ceremonies. Most visited of all were the neolithic stone circles of Castlerigg and Long Meg and her Daughters. Aubrey Burl, a twentieth century authority on megalithic circles, described Castlerigg Stone Circle as 'the most exciting and the most mysterious of all the superb rings in the Lake District.' It was the sense of awe and mystery which drew so many Georgian and Victorian tourists to the ancient monument in its magnificent mountain setting.[16]

Long Meg has always presented the puzzle of precisely how many daughters she has. Legend has it that the stones were

Mayborough Henge, John Aubrey: 'A great circular Bank of stones and earth with four stones of great magnitude.'

Long Meg and her daughters. The third largest stone circle in Britain.

witches caught indulging in a ritual to which a thirteenth century wizard took exception and he turned them into stone. They can only be released if someone is able to count the correct number of stones twice in succession. This, it is alleged, has yet to be done although many have tried: 'authoritative' versions vary between 59 and 77, an intriguing tourist attraction.

Similarly endowed with the virtue of antiquity were the ancient yew trees of the Lake District and they attracted numerous curious visitors. The Borrowdale Yews, celebrated in Wordsworth's verse, were still, in the eighteenth century and for most of the nineteenth century, a largely undamaged grove (a storm in 1883 inflicted great damage) and at 2,000 years of age were among the oldest trees in the country; the Patterdale Yews which had stood in the churchyard for well over a thousand years attracted many visitors, but they, too, were victims of the 1883 tempest; the Lorton Yew, also the subject of a Wordsworth eulogy, was renowned as the 'pulpit' from which the Quaker, George Fox, had addressed an assembled multitude. The few tourists who ventured into remote Martindale stood in awe before the yew tree by St Martin's Church, already more than 1,000 years old when the Christians first came here.

Mysteries of any kind, particularly if they have a whiff of the supernatural associated with them, have always had an audience and visitors to the Lake District were not disappointed. One phenomenon

The Lorton Yew – Edwin Bogg – 'Two thousand miles of wandering' 1888 where he describes the tree as 'only a wreck of its former glory.'

aroused special interest because it was alleged to have occurred almost within living memory of Regency tourists: this was the phantom army of Souther Fell, a high ridge in a loop of the River Glenderamackin, north-east of Keswick. On three occasions, in 1735, 1737 and 1745, local inhabitants witnessed a large army marching from north to south across the summit of the fell and disappearing over the horizon. This was seen by twenty-six people but no marks of any kind could be found on the turf At that time a possible meteorological explanation had not been put forward, but the date 1745 and the invasion of Bonnie Prince Charlie still, 50 years later, carried a fearful resonance in England.[17]

Windermere boatmen, rowing a captive group of visitors on

the scenic trip round the islands, had in their repertoire of tales a ghost story to strike fear into any timid tourists, some already apprehensive perhaps about being out in a frail craft on this vast lake of unquiet waters. A short distance north of Belle Isle on the west side of the lake is the haunt of the only ghost to be identified on an Ordnance Survey map. This is the Crier of Claife whose story was no doubt suitably embellished for tourist consumption, but is told succinctly by Harriet Martineau who sets it in the sixteenth century:

> It was about the time of the Reformation, one stormy night, when a party of travellers were making merry at the Ferryhouse ... a call for the boat was heard from the Nab. A quiet, sober boatman obeyed the call, though the night was wild and fearful. When he ought to be returning, the tavern guests stepped out upon the shore to see whom he would bring. He returned alone, ghastly and dumb with horror. Next morning he was in a high fever, and in a few days he

The Three Shires Stones, 1852, by T. L. Aspland. The original three stones marked with the initial letters of the counties of Cumberland, Westmorland and Lancashire.

died, without having been prevailed upon to say what he had seen at the Nab. For weeks after, there were shouts, yells and howlings at the Nab on every stormy night: and no boatman would attend to any call after dark.[18]

(More recent sightings appear to confirm that the ghost is that of a sixteenth century monk ...)[19]

The lake trippers were no doubt greatly relieved when their boatman rowed them round the other side of Belle Isle to visit two of Thomas West's 'stations' for the best views along the lake, and to join in the general condemnation of the recent (1774) construction there by a Mr English of a large circular house and formal gardens quite inappropriate to the island's natural setting. William Gilpin's guidebook informed visitors that 'the proprietor spent six thousand pounds upon it; with which sum he has contrived to do almost everything that one would wish had been left undone', while Thomas West expressed the hope that 'it will be

Windermere with Storrs Temple and Storrs House,
early nineteenth century.

100

Windermere from Low Wood.

his pleasure ... to restore the island to its native state of pastoral simplicity and rural elegance.' William Gell memorably pronounced that the round house 'wants only a little green paint and a label of Souchong or fine Hyson to make it exactly like a large shop tea canister.'[20]

Patriotic tourists would surely have persuaded their boatman to take them to see the new viewing 'station' built in 1804 to honour the great British naval victories of the eighteenth century. Enjoying magnificent views along the lake this small stone structure, known as Storrs Temple, bears the names of four of the outstanding admirals of the time: Duncan, Howe, Nelson and St Vincent.

Adventurous and energetic tourists braved the rough, intimidating (or thrilling) track through Langdale to the summit of Wrynose Pass to demonstrate their physical dexterity at the Three Shires Stones. These three stones, described as being 'of the size of a high-crowned hat' – about five feet distant from each other –

and forming a triangle had marked the boundaries of the three counties of Cumberland, Westmorland and Lancashire probably since the thirteenth century. Their interest as a tourist attraction lay perhaps less in their topographical significance than in their possibilities as a piece of gymnastic apparatus. A. C. Gibson, among others, describes the exercise:

> If you are tolerably lish and lengthy of limb, you may place a foot upon one stone, the other foot on another, and your hands on a third, or should the circumstances under which you visit the spot require you to do the feat more decorously, you may place both feet on one stone and distribute your hands between the other two; either way you perform it you may brag thereafter that you have been in three counties at one and the same time.[21]

The early tourists had no cameras to record the places they had visited but the affluent among them could take home a selection of the many watercolours on sale in artists' galleries in Keswick or Ambleside while the less wealthy could choose from the numerous prints and engravings of most of the beauty spots, waterfalls, historical sites, curiosities and scenes of romantic legend. It was perhaps just as well that no pictorial record was ever made of a certain fellside reflection in Ullswater noted by Coleridge, a droll caprice of Nature which he chose to describe a little obscurely as a 'weiblich tetragrammaton', adding that he 'never saw so sweet an Image ...'[22]

8

CRINOLINES SWELLING ON THE MOUNTAINS

THE young ladies of Jane Austen's novels, who represented the minor gentry of that Regency age, had little to do except retail the latest gossip, practise their needlecraft and piano-playing or excitedly anticipate the arrival of a letter or a visit from a neighbouring gentleman. They might also read together the latest Gothic horror from Mrs Radcliffe or lose themselves in the latest romance from Sir Walter Scott, but physical exercise, except dancing, was frowned on. When Elizabeth Bennet decided to walk the three miles to Netherfield 'crossing field after field at a quick pace, jumping over stiles and springing over puddles with impatient activity, and finding herself at last within view of the house, with weary ankles, dirty stockings, and a face glowing with the warmth of exercise', Mrs Hurst and Miss Bingley 'held her in contempt for it.'[1] And Wordsworth felt impelled to write a poem of

Ladies' walking dress circa 1810, from Ellen Weeton's Journal

103

consolation and encouragement to 'A Young Lady who had been reproached for taking a walk in the country.'

It is, therefore, gratifying to discover that there were many spirited young ladies of that time who were happy to venture into the 'wild, barren and frightful country' of the Lake District. In their long, flowing skirts, Roman boots and fashionable bonnets, they climbed the highest peaks, toiling over rough and stony tracks and struggling through boggy mires to reach summits then rarely trodden except by local shepherds, or they would endure long, uncomfortable rides in a ponycart or wagonette, and miles of rough walking, to visit remote valleys or isolated waterfalls – and afterwards produce shrewd, critical – and often lyrical – descriptions of all that they had seen.

Dorothy Wordsworth and her friend Mary Barker, 'an active climber of the hills', climbed Scafell Pike in 1818 by way of Sprinkling Tarn and Esk Hause, enjoyed a hearty picnic on the summit, endured a sharp, fierce rainstorm which produced multiple rainbows, descended by Styhead Tarn, and returned to Seathwaite in the moonlight.

Dorothy's description of the summit plateau of Scafell Pike is not only a delightful piece of English prose, but is also a reminder of how the passage of time and thousands of boots can change the landscape:

> ...not a blade of grass was to be seen – hardly a cushion of moss, and that was parched and brown and only growing rarely between the huge blocks and stones which cover the summit and lie in heaps all around to a great distance, like skeletons and bones of the earth not wanted at the creation, and there left to be covered with never-dying lichen, which the clouds and the dew nourish; and adorn with colours of the most vivid and exquisite beauty, and endless in variety. No gems or flowers can surpass in colouring the beauty of some of these masses of stone which no human eye ever beholds except

the shepherd led thither by chance or traveller by curiosity; and how seldom this must happen'.[2]

However, Dorothy Wordsworth was not a 'tourist'. A brief comment in her Journal for 9 June 1800, inplies that she would probably be mildly amused to be so described: 'A coronetted Landau went by, when we were sitting on the sodded wall. The ladies (evidently Tourists) turned an eye of interest upon our little garden and cottage.'[3]

There were, of course, many tourists at this time – coronetted or not – who came to the Lake District merely to gape at the beauty and shudder at the horror they had read about in the accounts of Thomas Gray or Thomas West or seen in numerous paintings or engravings. These were the tourists who earned the wrath of William Green in his *New Tourists Guide* of 1818: 'What enjoyment can be experienced by those who, lolling in their chariots, confine themselves to glimpses to be obtained from their windows?'[4] There were many others, however, who did not deserve such strictures, among them a number of adventurous, cultured and observant 'ladies of quality'.

Charlotte Brontë regretted that her enjoyment of her brief visit to the Lake District was diminished by being confined to her host's carriage: 'If I could only have dropped unseen out of the carriage, and gone away by myself in amongst those grand hills and sweet dales, I should have drunk in the full power of this glorious scenery.'[5]

In 1802 Mary Lamb had few problems in ascending Skiddaw with her brother Charles, but nearly thirty years later Edward Baines and his companion insisted that such a climb would be too exhausting for the ladies in their party who had to be provided with ponies and it was decreed that 'George and I were to walk at their sides for their security.' The ladies were left behind when

Edward and George set off to climb Helvellyn, the ascent being 'too perilous', an arrangement which would not have suited the novelist, Mary Elizabeth Braddon who took the 'perilous' climb in her stride and sat on the 'topmost point of the mountain' looking 'feebly at the Striding Edge, a narrow and precipitous spur which juts out from the main bulk of Helvellyn', noting the 'points from which divers aspiring souls have been hurled to eternity.' She added with dry humour, 'Sheep appear to like it, but that is their affair; and the fact that they are better as mutton makes one indulgent to their absurdity; but that humanity should be forever yearning to explore regions in which it has to sprawl, cling and clamber like a fly on a ceiling, is surely a subject for mild wonder.'[6]

Dorothy Wordsworth climbed Helvellyn many times and exclaimed at the 'glorious, glorious sights. The sea ... the Scottish mountains ... Mists above and below, and close to us, with the Sun amongst them.'[7]

Then there was Elizabeth Smith, a young, gifted scholar, admired by De Quincey as 'eminently accomplished', 'a most extraordinary person.' Her health was undermined by tuberculosis but she was a determined climber of the fells and, in 1805, just a year before her death at the age of 30, she and her sisters invited the guidebook writer Thomas Wilkinson, to accompany them to the top of Helvellyn. Wilkinson declined as he was fearful of having to negotiate 'wreaths of snow and sheets of ice', but the young ladies 'ridiculed my effeminacy, telling me that they had all three made the summit without a guide.' The Smith sisters did succeed in persuading Wilkinson to join them on an expedition to the Langdale Pikes but their progress was clearly too slow for Elizabeth who went ahead to explore the summits alone. Her absence from the rest of the party 'was terribly extended' an alarmed Wilkinson wrote, 'I knew not whether she might be climbing up

Striding Edge, Helvellyn, Geoffrey Berry.

the cliffs above us, or falling down the precipice below ... but we were at length relieved by her calling to us from the cliffs over our heads.' A year later she died.[8]

Another independent young lady of these times was Ellen Weeton, Governess at Dove Nest between 1809 and 1811. She escaped from her unpleasant employer by venturing into the hills and participating in any local tourist activities. Her Journal reveals a lively, independent personality, determined not to be confined by the conventions surrounding her gender and her vocation. In the spring of 1810 she and the footman often 'took the boat ourselves, he at one oar and myself at the other, for several miles down the lake; and one morning I went in a small row boat round one of the islands alone.'

Later in the summer she joined a party to climb Fairfield in a 'bitter cold wind' and on reaching the summit they 'sat down upon the ground, and enjoyed a hearty meal of veal, ham, chicken, gooseberry pies, bread, cheese, butter, hung leg of

Stockley Bridge with walkers, 1824, by W. Green.

mutton, wine, porter, rum, brandy, and bitters.' A hearty picnic indeed, and, not surprisingly, we learn that all this was carried up the fell by a donkey. 'When our hunger was appeased, we began to stroll about and enjoy the extensive prospect. We had several prospect glasses, and the air was very clear. I was much pleased, though awed by the tremendous rocks and precipices in various directions.'[9]

Miss Weeton was clearly made in a different mould from the demure, diffident, self-effacing governess so often portrayed in literature. Her account of one of the 'foot races' during the Windermere Regatta verges on the Rabelaisian:

Two of them ran without shirts; one had breeches on, the other only drawers ... Expecting they would burst or come off, the ladies durst not view the race, and turned away from the sight. And well it was they did, for during the race, and with the exertion of running, the drawers did actually burst, and the man cried out as he run – 'O Lord! O Lord! I cannot keep my tackle in, G-dd-n it! I cannot keep my tackle in.' The ladies, disgusted, every one left the ground; there were many of fashion and rank … but all trooped off.[10]

Miss Weeton seems to have followed 'the ladies' as she adds, 'Wrestling and leaping occupied the remainder of the day, we were told'.

Some fifty years after Ellen Weeton's adventures there arrived in 'The Lake Country', perhaps

Dorothy Wordsworth

Eliza Lynn Linton.

the most formidable of all the female tourists of this period, a young woman with keen and shrewd powers of observation, literary gifts, inexhaustible curiosity, deep appreciation of the beauty of the natural landscape, and resources of fearless energy which took her to almost every corner of the area from the depths of a Langdale quarry to the tops of the highest fells. She was Eliza Lynn Linton, granddaughter of Samuel Goodenough, Bishop of Carlisle, and so a 'lady of high quality', even though her husband was a chartist and republican.

She was the first to appreciate the gentle serenity and charm of Bassenthwaite and among the few who made the strenuous journey to the remote valleys of Wasdale and Ennerdale whose wild, lonely and austere grandeur is still very much as she described it. Her style was far removed from the emotionally charged hyperbole of many contemporary visitors: she interpreted the scenery with a rational clarity which in no way diminished her sensitive appreciation.

William Gilpin, visiting Ullswater, declared that he 'had seen nothing so beautifully sublime, so correctly picturesque as this'; Mrs Linton saw it as possessing 'a certain savageness and solitude'; she portrayed the now polished and respectable village of Troutbeck as a 'picturesque, wild, dirty and diseased' bye-hamlet which, she prophetically added, would 'in a few years ... be cleaned, schooled and ornamented, and made fit-company for ambitious Windermere and respectable Ambleside.' Nor did she share the ecstasy usually bestowed on the cascades in the grounds of Rydal Hall which she considered to be

...so pretty and well-arranged that surely their fittest place is the back scene of some pastoral opera ... the trees have been so artistically disposed – the vistas so cunningly contrived – the channels have been so scientifically deepened – the resting-basin so tastefully arranged – and the summer-house is such a bit of picturesque trick, that one loses all perception of nature, and cannot but regard these very elegant waterfalls as artificial altogether.[11]

By contrast she was very much moved by the genuine warmth, hospitality and comfortable domesticity she experienced when she called at a Lakeland farmhouse to ask for refreshment during

Thrang Crag slate quarry, Langdale, T. Allom, 1834. The gaping caverns and enormous excavations of the Lakeland slate quarries featured in some of the early guide books and were visited by many tourists. Eliza Lynn Linton gave a vivid description of her visit to Thrang Crag.

one of her many long walks; and she was full of admiration for the quarrymen of Honister as she watched them at their dangerous work. Her astonished wonder did not prevent her from noting the many unusual plants which grow in the crevices and gullies on these brooding crags. She was probably the first 'tourist' to appreciate that the Lake District is a place where people make their homes and earn a livelihood and an integral area of natural beauty not a collection of picturesque beauty spots.[12]

Eliza Lynn Linton was also a bold and intrepid walker. Her enthusiastic description of her 'many and beautiful walks about Ambleside' which 'all but very fine ladies or very delicate ones, may take without too much fatigue,'[13] is put into context when she writes of 'a delicious day's walk of only twenty-six miles in all' – a casual comment recalling Sarah Aust's relaxed account of her stay in Buttermere in 1796: 'One day I walked over the mountains by Gatesgarth into Ennerdale, and through it to Ennerdale Bridge, on the whole, sixteen miles.'[14] As the Hon. Mrs Murray, Sarah was celebrated as the 'First Lady of Quality to cross Honister Pass.'

Mrs Linton's guide to an expedition to Loughrigg Fell reads like a challenge to any young and spirited Victorian lady:

> Walls must be clambered over, and rough gates and stiles everywhere; and where you are sure to find yourselves in places in which you have no earthly business to be; but you will finally set yourselves straight, and strike the right road for a pathless scramble over the fell.

Similarly, her account of a visit to Scale Force, a remote but popular attraction at the time, indicates the sturdy, adventurous character of her young contemporaries:

Ennerdale Water, T. Allom, 1832. The few tourists who ventured as far as Ennerdale saw it as Thomas Allom portrayed it – craggy and bare of trees. Eliza Linton found Ennerdale 'wild, lonely and austere; at the head wonderfully noble, with a majesty of mountain unusual. But it is not lovely.'

It is pleasant among these slippery rocks, where, if you do plunge knee-deep in the pools, you come to no vital harm, and can shake yourself from the wet out on the spongy bit of waste-land, stone-strewed, leading from the Force to the lake. Mishaps, if not too serious, only add to the enjoyment; and he is a bastard mountaineer who cannot take a ducking with unruffled equanimity.[15]

However, it is in her ascent of the high fells that Eliza so totally repudiates the weak and vapid female of Victorian literary convention.

'Never take the gentler way,' she proclaims, 'but up the very face of these wild ... crags, the true rocky scramble'; for her, 'the heroic way from Keswick to Ullswater is straight over Helvellyn' and her recommended route up Blencathra 'is not always a pleasant track to walk in, especially when the wind blows with such force that you may be blown fairly over.'[16] Most remarkable of all is the account she gives of her climb from Mardale to the summit of High Street, an ascent of well over 2,000 feet in three miles by what Alfred Wainwright called 'the connoisseurs' route', not 'the gentler way' at all:

...small footholds ... loose stones and slanting slides ... a set of steps a yard high and sometimes overgrown with slippery grass ... gaps through which nothing larger than a lean lamb could force itself, are sometimes the only way of passing from a lower ground to a higher unless you can drag yourself up the cleft by mere force of arms or shoulders, or the weakest be dragged up by the stronger ... The sharp angles will graze you, the gorse will tear your ancles and the juniper will prick your hands; and ever the climb grows steeper and the way more rugged, ever the need of going on without halting or daring to look over or below ... till with a supreme effort, scrambling up a narrow ledge where one slip of the hand or foot would be simple death, you get over the last barrier and stand on the broad turfed down which is the top of High Street.[17]

By 1860 ladies' walking dress was certainly less voluminous than it had been a generation earlier: Mrs Linton herself wrote dismissively of 'life long ago' with 'crinolines swelling on the mountains'.[18] Even so one wonders how this rocky scramble was negotiated at all encumbered by those flowing Victorian skirts and petticoats.

This indomitable daughter of the Cathedral Close also made the ascent of Great Gable and Scafell Pike and wrote delightful vignettes of both mountains. Great Gable, she noted, is

> ...hollowed in the centre and buttressed with grey pillars on each side – a whole cascade of immense boulders pouring from that sweeping curve to show what wind and rain have done, and the jewelled brightness of its sides shining many coloured and glorious if the sun lights on them ... It is one of the finest mountains to ascend; giving some of the grandest views and most glorious effects.[19]

On the summit plateau of Scafell Pike she rejoiced in the colourful lichens which had delighted Dorothy Wordsworth sixty years before: 'lichens as brilliant and gorgeous as if they had been garden beds of flowers or clusters of precious stones.'[20]

Her description of the view from Scafell Pike at sunset epitomises the sensitive and almost poetic interpretation of the natural beauty of the Lakeland scene composed by so many of these hardy feminine explorers of the dales and fells:

> ...Wastwater lay dark and broken below, and two little tarns beyond it; a sparkle was on Kirkfell, and Mosedale and Black Sail looked full of purple ripeness; the sun had caught a portion of Crummock lake till it glowed like a cup of red wine spilled on the earth ... the sun was sinking, leaving long bars of red and gold, and a tender, mellow glory everywhere, like a calm of prayer for all England ...

She and her companions then calmly settled down to spend the

Ullswater, by J. Harwood, 1849, a popular tourist attraction. Wordsworth considered it to be 'perhaps the happiest combination of beauty and grandeur which any of the Lakes affords', and Gilpin wrote that 'we had seen nothing so beautifully sublime, so correctly picturesque as this.'

night on the summit of England's highest mountain:

> We made our beds of the flattest stones we could find and agreed to wait patiently for the morning. The only sound was that of the winds which shouted like thunder as at last they saw us to sleep in the continuing twilight.[21]

Eliza Lynn Linton and her contemporary 'tourists' had demonstrated that it was possible for 'ladies of quality' to enjoy strenuous walks and climb the Lakeland fells without (as she herself put it) 'the necessity for a fit of apoplexy half-way.'

9

ALIVE AND SWARMING WITH TOURISTS

IN 1778 the *Monthly Magazine* reported that 'To make a tour of the Lakes, to speak in fashionable language, is the *ton* of the present hour.' By 1800 Samuel Taylor Coleridge, then residing at Greta Hall in Keswick, complained, no doubt with some exaggeration, that for a third of the year the Lake District was alive and swarming with tourists. By 1820 travel had become cheaper for those who could afford it, faster and more comfortable following the great improvements in road construction using the techniques introduced by John McAdam and Thomas Telford.

This was the hey-day of the stage coach; regular services with published fares and timetables were in place to all parts of the country; important advances had been made in coach design, especially with the development of springs to minimise the jolts on uneven roads; a fast strong horse, the Cleveland Bay, had been bred to pull the heavy vehicles over long distances; and, in many counties, inns had greatly improved their facilities to meet the expectations of their upper class guests. Travelling to satisfy the new curiosity about Britain, its landscape, its history, its industrial wonders, its myths and legends, and above all, at that time, its wild and mountainous regions, had become a pleasurable activity, an antidote to the increasingly squalid and corrupt life in the towns and cities.

Lakeland was frequented by more and more tourists in the early decades of the nineteenth century and, as we have seen, various 'attractions' were soon introduced to entertain them when they tired of their guidebook tours of the beauty spots and scenic

Wray Castle, W. Banks.

wonders. These tourists were birds of passage, returning home after a few weeks or so with their journals and diaries and prints of the sights they had seen: they were holiday makers on the fashionable 'tour of the Lakes.'

The early decades of the nineteenth century also brought a very different type of 'off-comers' to the district. They came to stay and change the landscape by buying carefully selected plots of land with fine scenic prospects on which they built imposing mansions, often architecturally eccentric and alien to the modest native buildings. In his *Guide to the Lakes* Wordsworth wrote scathingly of these intrusive structures:

No one can now travel through the frequented tracts, without being offended, at almost every turn, by an introduction of discordant objects and disturbing that peaceful harmony of form and colour, which had been through a long lapse of ages most happily preserved.[1]

117

Allan Bank – illustration from a 1911 sale notice.

These new 'settlers' were largely drawn from the newly affluent and socially ambitious industrial and mercantile middle classes or from the professional and academic ranks of Regency and Victorian society. They did not necessarily feel any special sensitivity to the Lakeland scene: as Wordsworth put it, their 'fancies were smitten', but they changed the lakeland landscape for ever.[2]

The shores of Windermere were transformed in these years. The absentee Bishop of Llandaff, Richard Watson, who managed to be simultaneously Professor of Divinity and Professor of Chemistry at Cambridge, considered the Tudor manor at Calgarth Hall unfitted to his dignity and built the uninspired Georgian house nearby known as Calgarth Park. His appreciation of his Lakeland domicile may be judged by his proposal to drain Windermere to create land for agriculture, a plan which he abandoned only when, as Ellen Weeton informs us, 'the expense of doing it would have greatly exceeded the advantage.'[3]

Storrs Hall was built by John Bolton, a Liverpool merchant

with a profitable interest in the slave trade; Belsfield, overlooking the lake at Bowness, was the home of Henry Schneider, the iron master, who was served breakfast each day on his yacht to Lakeside train station from where he travelled in his own compartment to Barrow-in-Furness to preside over the largest ironworks in the world; Brathay Hall was the home of John Harden, the landscape painter; James Dawson, a Liverpool surgeon, was responsible for Wray Castle, largely paid for by his wife's fortune derived from the manufacture of gin and generally ridiculed as a 'pantomime set-piece'; the famous round house on Belle Isle was the creation of Mr English who was universally condemned for all that he did on the island but it was happily bought a few years later by Isabella Curwen, heiress to the mining fortunes of the Curwens of Workington; Sir James Kay-Shuttleworth, the educationalist and textile tycoon, rented Briery Close, and John Wilson (also known as Christopher North) Professor of Moral Philosophy at Edinburgh, built a holiday home at Elleray, where, on one notable occasion, he covered the floor of the main reception room with turf in order to stage a cock-fight; Dove Nest, originally a simple eighteenth century cottage, was transformed by Edward Pedder, the wealthy but unpleasant son of a Preston banker. (Ellen Weeton was governess here when she wrote her lively journal; and the poetess, Felicia Hemans, lived here from 1829-31.)

In Grasmere the most desirable site was bought by a Liverpool lawyer, John Crump, who in 1805 built Allan Bank with its wonderful panoramic view into the Vale of Grasmere. Its construction was met with much local opposition not least from the Wordsworths who found its pink walls directly in their view from Dove Cottage: Wordsworth described it as 'a temple of abomination' which 'will stare you in the face from every part of the Vale, and entirely destroy its character of simplicity and seclusion.'

Local builders were also disgruntled that Crump should show such distrust of their skills that he brought in builders from Liverpool and there was much mildly malicious laughter when the completed walls suddenly collapsed and all had to be rebuilt. Within three years Wordsworth had apparently changed his mind for in 1808 he and his growing family took up residence at Allan Bank but only for three years as they were unable to solve or tolerate the problem of 'smoky chimneys' which affected almost every room. Allan Bank was obviously not an architectural success.[4]

A few miles away, Dr Arnold, Headmaster of Rugby School, built a holiday home at Fox How, a house much more to Wordsworth's prescription for he took an almost possessive interest in its design, insisting on the Westmorland vernacular style of round chimneys, unrendered stone walls and traditional porch. Arnold's grand-daughter, Mrs Humphry Ward, the novelist, described Fox How as 'a modest building, with ten bedrooms and three sitting rooms.' Dr Arnold apparently had little interest in the special recreational opportunities of his Lakeland environment for he admonished his exploring children with the opinion that 'mere mountain and lake hunting was time lost.'[5]

Far to the south of this central tourist area, but a familiar sight to those brave enough to enter the Lake District by the sands crossing, stands the Gothic fantasy of Conishead Priory. Built on the site of a twelfth century religious foundation destroyed at the Dissolution, the present house was the work of Colonel Bradyll, who made and lost his fortune in the Durham coalfields. Although intended to be a private residence it was designed as if it was still a Priory with a monastic-style gatehouse, seats like choir stalls and passages reminiscent of cloisters, perfectly reflecting that fascination with medieval romanticism which so influenced artistic taste for much of the nineteenth century.

Conishead Priory, circa 1830, E. Waugh, Rambles in the Lake Country.

It was built at the end of the Georgian period and from its early days it appeared in the tourist guidebooks, even, surprisingly, in Wordsworth's own *Guide to the Lakes*, for it is as far removed from the poet's idea of homely architecture as one can imagine. Norman Nicholson gave a colourful description of the sight which would greet the unsuspecting tourist: 'From a distance it holds to the sky a roof-line as cluttered and complicated as a fretwork pipe-rack – square towers, crochet-worked turrets; spikes, pinnacles and pimples; crenellated balustrades, crow-stepped gables, twisted and twiddly chimneys.'[6]

Wealth from industry also enabled the Marshall family, flax-spinners from Leeds, to acquire a number of estates in the area, notably Derwent Island, Monk Coniston, 2,000 acres at the northern end of Derwentwater (including Friar's Crag which Wordsworth, in a stupefying aberration or with tongue in cheek, suggested would be an ideal site to build a mansion), and

Patterdale Hall by Ull-swater.

This Italianate house, designed by Anthony Salvin, and the elaborately laid-out gardens were in marked contrast to the 'palace' of the Moun-sey family, self-styled Kings of Patterdale who 'reigned' here be-fore. John Mounsey, 93 in 1795, was one of Lakeland's notable ec-centrics and a great tourist attraction. James Clarke, William Gilpin, John Hous-man, Joseph Bud-worth, Dorothy Wordsworth all recorded entertaining accounts of their visits to the Mounsey house-hold, Dorothy claim-ing that the 'Queen' was driven to drink by the antics of the 'King'.[7]

Above, Thomas De Quincey, and below, Robert Southey.

John Ruskin.

Many a tourist must have returned home armed with extraordinary tales of Lakeland characters such as John Mounsey, Peter Crosthwaite, Joseph Pocklington, and even Harriet Martineau – although it is doubtful if anyone caught sight of her walking the Kirkstone road at five o'clock in the morning or bathing naked in the grave-like rainwater-pool she had dug out in her garden. The new 'off-comers' stood apart from the 'natives' and valued their seclusion too much to appreciate the prying eyes of the 'tourist'.

The Lake District was steadily being colonised by these settlers and the landscape changed by their imposing mansions strung out along the lake shores. At the same time an entirely different class of settler was beginning to haunt the area and particularly Derwentwater and the town of Keswick. These were the 'Lake Poets', all – except Wordsworth – new comers who were never assimilated into local society but remained a group apart, a tight social circle but famous enough as literary figures to be known to most tourists. In a sense, they were the celebrities of the time.

It was with some justification that Percy Bysshe Shelley, writing in 1821, could declare that poets were the unacknowledged

Greta Hall.

legislators of the world, for he was writing at a time when poets held a place in the thoughts and opinions of the educated classes which today we find difficult to comprehend. The various tracts, pamphlets and newspapers circulating in the clubs, coffee houses and town residences often cited poetry to adorn their text, and even parliamentary debates were liberally embellished with apt quotations, not only from the classics but also from contemporary poets.

Members of the Royal Society and the Dilettanti Club, and even of such clubs as Almack's, Boodles and Brooks were expected to contribute to conversations on the latest volume of poetry or current exhibitions by Turner, Constable or Reynolds. In the literate society of the Georgian period 'intellectual many sidedness was expected and respected.'[8] This cultural elite was no more than a tiny fraction of the population, but it set the *ton* for the gentry and the rising middle class: Henry Fielding, perhaps referring mischievously to the 1,200 guests who frequented the balls and receptions at Devonshire House, commented that 'Nobody' was 'all the people in Great Britain except about 1,200.'[9]

In the decades between 1770 and 1830 the *ton* demanded an attachment to the Romantic Movement. This was a reaction against the classic rationalism which had dominated much of the eighteenth century in almost every field of intellectual and artistic endeavour. It was a reaction, also, against a world increasingly dominated by science, by industrialisation, by the unsightly spread of mill and mining towns and by the loss of common land and open landscapes to the 'fearful symmetry' of enclosed fields. The rural idyll of Man and Nature working together in close proximity and mutual understanding was being replaced by the subjugation and exploitation of Nature by Man for his own material needs. The Romantics sought to discover in Nature Wordsworth's 'sense sublime of something far more deeply interfused' in the belief that:

> *One impulse from a vernal wood*
> *May teach you more of man,*
> *Of moral evil and of good,*
> *Than all the sages can.*

The poets of the 'Augustan age' with their heavy burden of classical references were no longer in fashion: the 'Romantic age' marked a seismic shift in attitudes to Nature. As we have already seen, literate society in the late eighteenth century found wild, untamed, mountainous landscape attractive where previously it had been shunned, and this was accompanied by a new appreciation of the natural world. The study of plants and flowers became an acceptable pastime for educated ladies. William Cowper lamented the loss of a group of poplar trees and public opinion was outraged when a forest of oaks was felled at the head of Derwentwater. For William Wordsworth,

> *...the meanest flower that blows can give*
> *Thoughts that do often lie too deep for tears,*

and John Keats was so overwhelmed by the splendour of Stock-ghyll Force that he exclaimed 'I shall learn poetry here'.

Jane Austen is a reliable guide to prevailing fashion among the gentry of her time and in *Sense and Sensibility*, published in 1811, a sisterly exchange between Elinor Dashwood and young Mari-anne discussing a visit by their new acquaintance, Willoughby, clearly suggests that popular opinion among the educated classes had fully embraced Romanticism and turned away from the 'Age of Reason':

> Well, Marianne, for one morning you have done pretty well. You have already ascertained Mr Willoughby's opinion on almost every matter of importance. You know what he thinks of Cowper and Scott; you are certain of his estimating their beauties as he ought, and you have received every assurance of his admiring Pope no more than is proper.[10]

The centre of the romantic movement was the Lake District where a circle of poets and other literary figures had gathered and become known as The Lake Poets, a misleading term in many re-spects for, as Thomas de Quincey himself pointed out, these poets came together only by accident or personal connection:

> ...the critics of the day supposed them to have assembled under common views in literature, particularly with regard to the true function of poetry and the true theory of poetic diction ... and went on to incorporate the whole community under the name of the Lakes School.[11]

Few of them lived in the Lakes for more than a short time and they could more accurately be described as 'tourists' for most of them produced little poetry inspired by the Lake District environ-ment and in their search for the picturesque revealed a lack of that deeper sensibility to Nature which was so important to Wordsworth.

Samuel Taylor Coleridge alone came closer to Wordsworth's poesy than any other of the Lakes Poets but even he observed the natural scene with the eye of a scientist describing what he saw in clinical detail, and almost always in prose. Much of his best poetry had already been written and he was painfully aware of his loss of true inspiration: his 'Ode on Dejection' mournfully reflects this:

> *It were a vain endeavour,*
> *Though I gaze forever*
> *On that green light that lingers in the west:*
> *I may not hope from outward forms to win*
> *The passion and the life, whose fountains are within.*

Yet the letters and journals he wrote describing his experiences on his marathon walking tours in Lakeland are vivid and compelling. His description of his adventures on Scafell Pike are perhaps best known but equally graphic are his impressions of a waterfall at Buttermere and of mist and sunlight on Derwentwater and Ullswater. Coleridge was probably the first 'tourist' to explore the fells – without guidebooks, compass or maps: his three great tours took him from Haweswater to Wastwater, from Keswick to St Bees, from Matterdale to Ennerdale, from Scafell to Skiddaw; and Dorothy Wordsworth noted in her 'Journal' Coleridge's moonlight walk to Grasmere from Keswick over Helvellyn:

At 11 o'clock Coleridge arrived while I was walking in the still, clear moonshine in the garden. He came over Helvellyn ... We sate and chatted till half past three, W. in his dressing gown, Coleridge read us a part of Christabel. Talked much about the mountains.[12]

Coleridge lived at Greta Hall, Keswick, for three years and struck up an easy acquaintance with numerous cottagers and farmers who provided him freely with food and drink on his lengthy walks in the mountains, a social skill never achieved by Wordsworth. By contrast Robert Southey who lived at Greta Hall for forty years remained aloof from the local population but welcomed a host of literary guests to Greta Hall and hauled them to the summit of Skiddaw or Great Gable to admire the view. Although appointed Poet Laureate in 1813 he produced little poetry of note during all his years in the Lake District but devoted almost all his time to the production of highly regarded biographies of Nelson, Wesley and Cowper, as well as numerous contributions to magazines and journals.

His industrious pen also produced the lively, brilliant *Letters from England* written under the assumed name of Don Manuel Alvarez Espriella, a Spaniard on a tour of England, who has many apt and sharp comments to make on English prejudices but also notes some of the absurdities of tourist attractions. His visit to the Bowder Stone inspired a particularly apposite and brisk description of the scene:

The same person *(i.e. Joseph Pocklington)* who formerly disfigured the island in Keswick Lake with so many abominations, has been at work here also; has built a little mock heritage, set up a druidical stone, erected an ugly house for a woman to live in who is to show the rock, for fear travellers should pass under it without seeing it, cleared away all the fragments round it, and as it rests upon a narrow base, like a ship upon its keel, dug a hole underneath through which the curious may gratify themselves by shaking hands with the old woman. The oddity of this amused us greatly, provoking as it was to meet with such hideous buildings in such a place, – for the place is as beautiful as eyes can behold or imagination conceive.[13]

Other literary celebrities of the time who came to live in the Lake District included John Wilson (Christopher North) and Thomas de Quincey, both minor poets with a pioneering urge to explore the area and absorb its scenic and spiritual delights, but there any similarity ends. Wilson was physically strong as well as intellectually gifted, able to combine the editorship of *Blackwood's Magazine* with the composition of critical essays and modest poetry, and the post of Professor of Moral Philosophy at Edinburgh with an energetic exploration of the whole of Lakeland and the organisation of wrestling matches, fishing expeditions with other Lakes Poets, and brilliant regattas on Windermere.

De Quincey, on the other hand, was a dreamer and opium addict and an ardent disciple of Wordsworth through whom he joined the social circle of Lakes literati and wrote elegantly of his experiences. His *Reminiscences of the Lake Poets* contains some of the best prose descriptions of Lake District scenery. His vignette of Easedale is moving in its simplicity:

> I have often thought, while looking with silent admiration upon this exquisite composition of landscape, with its miniature fields, running up like forest glades into miniature woods; its little columns of smoke, breathing up like incense to the household gods, from the hearths of two or three picturesque cottages – abodes of simple primitive manners, and what, from personal knowledge, I will call humble virtue – I have thought that, if a scene on this earth could be deserved to be sealed up, like the valley of Rasselas, against the intrusions of the world – if there were one to which a man would willingly surrender himself a prisoner for the years of a long life – this is it – this Easedale – which would justify the choice and recompense the sacrifice.[14]

Hovering in a drunken haze on the fringes of this literary coterie was Hartley Coleridge, son of Samuel Taylor Coleridge. His erratic behaviour and his addiction to alcohol dimmed his talent as a poet but he managed to produce a few memorable lines which occasionally appear in anthologies.

More obviously a tourist was John Keats who came to the Lake District on a walking tour in 1818. He stayed at the inns which were slowly learning to meet the needs of this new breed of customer but, according to Keats, still had some way to go.

He wrote lively accounts of Stockghyll Force, Castlerigg Circle, and the Falls of Lodore (where as so often there were no falls to be seen) and clearly enjoyed his experience of a Cumberland 'merry neet'. He even got up at four o'clock to make a dawn ascent of Skiddaw. Like so many tourists he called at Rydal Mount hoping to see Wordsworth, only to find the great man out, but, surprisingly, he did not call at Greta Hall in Keswick where he would have been almost certain to find Robert Southey entertaining a few fellow poets. Keats produced no great poetry directly related to his tour of Lakeland but it is possible that he did find inspiration here and that his words at Stockghyll Force – 'I shall learn poetry here and henceforth write more than ever' – were prophetic, for in the months following his return to London he wrote much of his most distinguished verse – 'The Eve of St Agnes', 'Isabella', 'Lamia', and some of the best Odes.

The Lakes tour became almost a social necessity for the literary figures of these years. A list of some of those who made the journey might serve as a kind of 'Who's Who' in English Literature of the first half of the nineteenth century: Matthew Arnold inherited Fox How from his father and spent vacations there; Thomas Carlyle joined Edward Fitzgerald and Alfred Lord Tennyson at Mirehouse, home of the Speddings, where the first drafts of *Morte d'Arthur* were read and discussed – Bassenthwaite is said to be the lake into whose waters Sir Bedivere flung Arthur's sword, Excalibur.

Sir Walter Scott made a number of tours to the Lake District, walking the fells with Wordsworth, Humphry Davy, John Lock-hart and John Wilson. His best novel, *Guy Mannering*, is set in the Border country, well to the north of the Lake District, but its great character, Meg Merrilies, was probably drawn from any one of the thousands of travellers who thronged the roads of Lakeland at that time, greatly outnumbering those visitors who came to admire the scenery.[15]

Charles Dickens was also on tour accompanied by Wilkie Collins collecting material for *Christmas Stories* and *The Lazy Tour of Two Idle Apprentices*; Percy Bysshe Shelley took a cottage in Keswick for three months and later stayed at Greystoke Castle as the guest of the Duke of Norfolk, but although he was enthusiastic about the scenery, he was not inspired to write any notable poetry; Elizabeth Gaskell frequently stayed in Silverdale on the southern edge of the Lake District where in the Tower House she worked on her novels, *Ruth* and *Sylvia's Lovers*; William Hazlitt, then intending to be an artist rather than a literary critic, paid a short visit to Keswick in 1803 with the purpose of painting portraits of Coleridge and Southey, but he left in a great hurry being chased out of the town by an angry mob after he allegedly assaulted a local girl who forcefully rebuffed his advances so, according to Wordsworth, 'he lifted up her petticoats and smote her on the bottom.' He fled to Dove Cottage where Coleridge gave him 'all the money I had in the world and the very Shoes off my feet to enable him to escape over the mountains.'

John Stuart Mill made the tour in 1831 and with his geologist's eye noted with obvious pleasure and fascination the various colours given to the cottages, barns, lakes and tarns by the different types of rock or slate and by the sunlight playing on them; the novelist, Barbara Hofland, widely read at the time but rarely heard of now, was a frequent guest at Mellfell House, under Little Mell Fell, and found there the inspiration to write one of her best known novels, *A Cumberland Statesman* vividly describing daily life on a prosperous Lakeland farm; Charles and Mary Lamb were guests of Coleridge at Greta Hall in 1802 and made the obligatory climb to the summit of Skiddaw where they were duly impressed by the 'prospect of mountains all about and about, making you giddy.'

Anthony Trollope and his mother had a fine house built near Penrith, but lived there 'one winter and half a summer' before deciding that 'the sun yoked his horses too far from Penrith town'; and a towering figure of the next generation, John Ruskin, was already, at the age of eleven, compiling a diary of sharply critical and astutely observant notes on all that he saw on his early tours round the Lake District – Wordsworth he found distinctly disappointing with his 'large nose with a moderate assortment of grey hairs and two small eyes' and a 'mouth large enough to let in a sufficient quantity of beef or mutton and to let out a sufficient quantity of poetry' and strongly disapproved of a group of women – 'oh, women indeed' – disfiguring the Derwent by washing linen in Derwentwater and hanging it on the boughs to dry.[16]

Two magnets drew these literary tourists to the Lake District in the first decades of the nineteenth century. The first was the passion for wild, mountain landscapes which enthralled the educated classes in these years; and the second was William Wordsworth whose published poems had by 1807 inspired a whole generation to see Nature as a healing force, a spiritual resource which neither the increasingly polluted and industrialised urban environment nor the uniform regularity of the newly fenced and hedged countryside could any longer provide.

10

FOREVER WADDLING TO THE WATERS

URBAN living, and especially life in London, in the eighteenth century could be an unhealthy experience. The air people breathed was polluted by domestic and industrial smoke; the water used for drinking, cooking and washing was often contaminated by sewage, industrial effluent and animal excretions; standards of personal and commercial hygiene were rudimentary, and, while food was becoming more plentiful, the diet of most of the population was unbalanced, fruit and green vegetables being largely shunned in favour of bread and cheese and, for those who could afford it, vast quantities of meat and poultry. A Cambridge professor of the time expressed the opinion that the goose was 'a silly bird – too much for one and not enough for two'.[1]

The upper classes of the time were notorious gluttons (the English gentry were known in Italy as *il populo del cinque pasti*, (the five-meals-a-day people) and much addicted to imbibing large quantities of claret, port and brandy. It is not at all surprising that so many of them suffered from disorders of the skin, dyspepsia, obesity, and other problems arising from a polluted environment, an unhealthy diet and unwise indulgence.

Medical science in the eighteenth century had made notable advances but it was an age of aspiration rather than actual achievement, and physicians and their patients, still turned to one of the most ancient of remedies for the troubles of their respiratory and digestive tracts and the diseases of their malnourished skins. It was fortuitous that these common hazards of urban life coincided with the contemporary urge to travel, and from the early eighteenth century a new brand of tourism gripped fashionable society and quickly spread to all parts of the country. This was the 'spa-cult' or 'taking the waters', an activity seized upon by the medical profession and their patients alike as the answer to almost any human ailment, both putting their faith in the impressive chemical analyses produced for almost every mineral spring in the country.

The fashionable world flocked to the spas to discover a remedy for their real or imagined illnesses but also to enjoy the company and diversions of a well-organised holiday. Health benefits came from the opportunity to drink clean water, to breathe clean air, and to enjoy a change of company and environment. The story of the English 'spa-cult' is well chronicled in a number of studies, journals and treatises and they leave no doubt that for some two hundred years this extraordinary craze gripped all those sections of society who could afford to indulge in it. Horace Walpole, as early as the mid-eighteenth century, was driven to observe that 'One would think the English were ducks; they are forever waddling to the waters'.

Celebrated spa resorts such as Bath, Cheltenham, Tonbridge, Leamington and Harrogate attracted large numbers of the aristocracy and the more affluent gentry and developed into elegant and prosperous towns. Almost every village in the land which could boast the existence of a mineral spring aspired to spa status and a few had their moment of glory but the keys to lasting success were ease of access, a wealthy clientele, medical publicity, and commercial enterprise to provide appropriate accommodation, entertainment facilities and a convincing but not too demanding regime of 'taking the waters'.

The remote and economically impoverished counties of the Lake District could never hope to emulate the more famous resorts but the geology of the area favoured an attempt to attract visitors by exploiting the wide variety of natural springs flowing from the rocks amid such inspiring scenery.

Saline, chalybeate and sulphur springs abounded in Cumbria and by the middle of the eighteenth century 23 of the 131 listed spas in England were found there.[2] In addition there were over 30 'Holy Wells' much frequented by local folk but too remote to achieve more than parochial fame and few of them impinged upon the curiosity of the Lakeland tourist. Other Lakeland 'spas' had a wider clientele, still almost largely northern and drawn from the minor gentry, but even so they contributed to the increase in the numbers of visitors to the area each year between June and October.

Such favoured spots included Humphrey Head where the waters were said to be identical with those of Cheltenham, Carlsbad and Baden-Baden; Witherslack, renowned, according to Thomas Short's 1766 *Treatise of Cold Mineral Waters*, for the treatment of, among other ailments, dropsy, worms, leprosy, corpulence and gravel; Short also pronounced that the saline spring at Manesty in Borrowdale would ensure 'a rough severe purge to a strong

Ruins of Stanger Spa, Vale of Lorton, Robert Gambles.

constituency', a testament which led to the provision of a bath-house on the site to accommodate visitors who apparently felt the need for this drastic therapy.[3]

Spas were found in remote and unlikely places and none more so than Gutterby Spa isolated on a lonely beach in south west Cumbria but even this was stated to be 'much frequented' and was 'a sovereign remedy for the scurvy and the gravel'.[4] The waters of Stanger Spa in the Vale of Lorton were similar to and as efficacious as those of Cheltenham and were well-patronised not only by the inhabitants of Cockermouth but also by visitors from further afield. Bottles of Stanger water were dispatched to other parts of the country and to distant places overseas.

Records of all these small spas in Lakeland are very sparse but since they were accorded the title of 'spa' it seems likely that they were much more widely known and visited than we would now imagine, for at that time the English were so addicted to the 'water cure' that it would be surprising if in the course of their 'tour of the Lakes' many tourists did not also take the opportunity to halt their coaches at these watering holes. (An informative and critical description of the spas in Cumbria may be found in *The Spas of England* by Dr August Bozzi Granville written in 1841 following a countrywide tour of most of the English spas frequented by the gentry at that time.)

Cumbria's two most successful spa resorts were located on the northern and eastern fringes of the Lake District, both in geographically unpromising sites for such establishments but both enjoying a flood of visitors for more than two centuries. Gilsland Spa was situated on the border with Northumberland almost within sight of Hadrian's Wall and on the banks of the River Irthing. Its sulphuretted waters had attracted visitors since Roman times and probably long before. Although the accommodation and facilities in 1840 were described as 'primitive' by Dr

Gilsland Spa, the promenade by the River Irthing, T. Allom, 1830s.

Granville, he clearly approved of the arrangements at the newly-built guest house called Shaws where there was a drawing room for the gentry, a stone-flagged parlour for 'the second class' and 'outhouses' for 'the poorer sort'.

There were three guest houses but they soon proved inadequate to accommodate the increasing number of visitors and by the 1860s a grandiose Spa Hotel had been built, equipped with all the latest Victorian furnishings and boasting all the facilities of much grander spas – dining rooms, drawing rooms, ladies' rooms, card rooms, billiard rooms, a quadrille band in the evenings, regular dress balls and a daily programme of recreation, entertainment and expeditions to the moors and to the Lake District. In the grounds were lawns for tennis, croquet and bowls, terraced walks leading down to the riverside where 'patients' would find book-stalls, bath-houses, refreshment huts and the fountain of the malodorous spa waters.

Gilsland Spa, the popping stone, Robert Gambles.

Gilsland could never rival the splendours of Bath or Cheltenham, but tourists flocked there from the northern counties and their correspondence reveals that a tour through the Lake District was part of their experience. Dr Granville believed that these northern gentry and industrial middle class were a different breed of tourist from the more sophisticated travellers from the south and, as he bluntly put it, they were 'very so-so classes of people' more in search of entertainment, lively company, a change of air, than a possible cure for their various ailments; for most of them the time was preferably spent drinking, (alcohol not spa water), eating, dancing, gambling and making love. One wonders if this was really so very different from Beau Nash's Bath.

Robert Burns, no doubt, found his stay at Gilsland thoroughly congenial. The visit of Sir Walter Scott in 1797 was a memorable occasion for it was here that he met a young lady 'than whom a lovelier vision could hardly be imagined' and within a few days a whirlwind romance resulted in Scott's proposal of marriage at the now famous 'popping stone', a massive boulder by the riverside. [5] Dr Granville rather ungallantly commented that 'Prudent mammas who are anxious to see their daughters speedily and well-settled in the world had better look to the Spas of England'.

Lowther Castle, T. Allom, 1830s.

Gilsland's rival in social and medical prestige as a spa resort was located in the bleak, chilly, rainswept moorlands of Shap. For almost a century gentry, the wealthy middle class and, no doubt, prudent mammas, journeyed from all parts of the country to Shap Wells, some perhaps lured by the Spa Handbook's emphasis on the proximity of the Earl of Lonsdale's Lowther Castle and its house-guests of famous and titled aristocrats; others came with a genuine faith that a course of the sulphurous waters there would, as the Spa Handbook claimed, be beneficial for their 'dyspepsia, liver disorders, nervous system, glandular swellings, cutaneous infections, rheumatism, scrofula, calculi, dropsy, lung problems and diseases of the skin'; and listless gentlewomen would be unable to resist the promise that the clear air and the Spa waters would inspire 'the whole frame with a new animation, giving to the blanched and cadaverous cheek the glow of health, and to the turgid and spiritless eye the sparkle of life and energy'.[6]

Shap Wells, the Spa Hotel.

And, after 1848, the Earl of Lonsdale's new Spa Hotel offered accommodation and cuisine which, according to Dr Granville, 'would not have disgraced a first-rate hotel in London ... and for cleanliness, abundance of furniture and contrivances, as well as for the excellency of the beds, far superior to most of them'. The arrival of the railway in 1848 enabled many more clients to travel with ease to Shap and for the next sixty years the seventy beds were not one too many. The appeal of Shap Wells may have had much to do with its relaxed approach to diet: here there was the customary medical 'advice' but no attempt to impose a strict dietary regime. Indeed the hotel handbook made it clear that the cuisine was designed to cater for all tastes and perceived requirements: 'Every delicacy of the season is supplied to tempt the weak, sickly stomach of the invalid or to gratify the more capricious one of the epicurean tourist or traveller.'[7]

The construction of an elegant well-head with a stone base believed to have been filched from Renaissance Florence,

Shap Wells, the well head, sketch by W. Reading.

the erection of a thirty foot high sculptured monument to commemorate the coronation of Queen Victoria and the planting of formal gardens and rhododendron groves gave the final touches to the transformation of a primitive watering-hole into a spa with much of the ambience and opulence of resorts of greater renown.

Dr Granville may have found the hotel at Shap worthy of the highest praise but he was less enthusiastic about the waters of the mineral spring there which had 'several little floating bodies whitish and milk-like suspended in it', rather like a 'weak solution of soap and water'. The smell of sulphur was 'very marked' and 'instantly after drinking a glass and a half (he) experienced headache and eructation of the sulphuretted gas', although he conceded that when the water was warmed it lost its unappealing aspects and lay 'more comfortably on the stomach'. The medical claims he regarded as 'too near an approach to poetical fancy' to be taken seriously. There were clearly many who disagreed with this judgement.

Shap Wells and Gilsland were some miles distant from the centre of the Lake District where most tourists preferred to stay and, with so much diversion and entertainment available on the spot, it is difficult to determine how much they contributed to the flow of tourists to the Lake District. Information on this is almost non-existent but it is worthy of note that the Spa Handbook mentions 'ease of access to the Lakes' as part of its publicity material. One cannot help but feel that an expedition to the lake and mountain scenery of Windermere, Ambleside or Keswick would for many of the guests be a pleasant change from the bleak moorlands of the Shap Fell country or the borderlands about Gilsland. One suspects, too, that unless one were fully committed to 'taking the waters' it would be a relief to escape for a while from the sulphurous exhalations graphically described by local inhabitants as 'train smoke mixed with bad eggs'.

The many thousands of gentlefolk, 'second class' citizens and 'so-so people' who flocked to the Lakeland spas throughout the eighteenth century and well into the twentieth form a little known but probably significant part of the tourist discovery of the Lake District in these years and brought modest economic prosperity to unlikely places.

11

I DO NOT WANT TO LET THEM SEE HELVELLYN WHILE THEY ARE DRUNK

IN 1843 Thomas Babington Macaulay expressed the view that 'The history of England is emphatically the history of progress'. At that very time England was witnessing perhaps the most far-reaching period of progress in its history – not all Englishmen welcomed it and many viewed it with suspicion and even open hostility. The coming of the railways was to affect almost every aspect of the nation's life and their construction has been described as 'the greatest physical achievement carried out by the human race within a comparatively short space of time'.[1] Yet opposition to the 'invasion' of the 'iron horse' was heard from all quarters and especially from landowners whose property would be crossed by the new railtracks and polluted by foul-smelling smoke, and also from those who felt their 'peace and tranquillity' would be threatened by the hordes of uncouth urban characters who would come by rail to harass the countryside.

Wordsworth certainly felt that his Lake District would suffer unacceptable 'molestation' from 'cheap trains pouring out their hundreds ... of the imperfectly educated classes' and when it was proposed to construct a branch line to Windermere and on to Ambleside and Grasmere and possibly Keswick, he wrote his famous letters to the *Morning Post* outlining his objections to the scheme and expressing his concerns about an invasion of Lakeland by the 'labouring classes' who had neither the education nor the cultural sensitivity to 'benefit from a more speedy access than they now

Windermere Station.

have to this beautiful region'.[2]

Wordsworth was realist enough to know that, however plausible his objections may be, 'the railway power ... will not admit of being materially counteracted by sentiment' and that a new and alarming phase of Lakeland tourism was about to begin. It is often claimed that it was Wordsworth's much publicised opposition which halted the construction of the railway beyond Windermere. It is much more likely that financial and economic problems were the decisive factors.

So as the railtracks came ever closer to the Lake District it seemed inevitable that the 'advance of the ten thousand would' bring 'noisy pleasure', 'pot houses and beer shops' and 'desecration of the Sabbath' to destroy the peace and tranquillity of the hills and dales. The poet even appealed to the mountains and rivers to 'protest against the wrong': 'Hear YE that whistle? I call on you to share the passion of a just disdain.'[3]

Wordsworth was not alone in his apprehensions about the

impact of the uneducated masses on the Lake District. John Ruskin expressed similar sentiments in even more explicit terms as he shuddered at the prospect of more 'taverns and skittle grounds' and the lake shores littered with 'broken ginger-beer bottles', adding that the intruders from 'our manufacturing towns' would 'be no more improved by contemplating the scenery (of the Lake District) than of Blackpool'.[4]

By 1846 the construction of the main line from Euston to Carlisle was completed and in the following year the branch line to Windermere was also in place. Within a short time the summer weekends saw several thousand passengers arrive at Windermere, a new township which grew from the hamlet of Birthwaite. For a time this transferred the main tourist centre from Keswick to Windermere and Bowness, but in 1865 with the opening of passenger services from Penrith to Keswick 1,200 visitors arrived at Keswick station on Easter Monday.

In the following year the first excursion trains brought some

The steam yacht 'Gondola', an early photograph, National Trust.

3-4,000 day-trippers travelling from Preston at a cost of 3/- for the return fare.[5] Even before this invasion of day visitors it was estimated that Keswick, with a population in 1851 of 2,618, had to cope with some 15,000 tourists in the summer season, while a similar number arrived in Windermere on excursion trains from Manchester, Liverpool, Leeds and other northern towns.

The less frequented district of Furness also felt the impact of the penetration of railways into the area. The editor of the local newspaper *The Grange Visitor* reflected general opinion in the town when he wrote that all the trippers who arrived on the excursion trains made life 'anything but healthy and pleasurable for quiet people, by their noisy delight at their brief escape from the wilderness of brick and mortar,' but added that 'Grange, like every other rising place, must pay the penalty of increased popularity, in constant and increasing incursions of trippers during the great holidays of the year' and must move with the times.[6]

In 1859 a short line was constructed to Coniston from Broughton-in-Furness on the newly opened Furness Railway and shortly afterwards a farther branch from Ulverston brought the railway to Lakeside on the southern tip of Lake Windermere. The former was primarily intended for the transport of copper from the local mines but when mining came to an end the line had to rely on tourist traffic to survive, the main attraction for the day-tripper being a leisurely sail on Coniston Water in the luxury yacht 'Gondola', first launched in 1859.

Lakeside, on the other hand, was from the beginning planned with the tourist in mind. Visitors arrived there to find a restaurant complete with an orchestra playing popular melodies and a long quay where three steamers were waiting to take them the length of the lake to Ambleside where a northern high tea was served. Here the party might meet members of another excursion which began at Blackpool and travelled by sea across Morecambe Bay

Furness Abbey, 1846 – D. Crosthwaite. The construction of the Furness Railway and the Furness Abbey Station Hotel made this a popular tourist destination.

to Barrow where the train took the party to Lakeside and to sail along the lake to Ambleside. The 'day-out in the Lakes' continued by wagonette or charabanc from Ambleside to Coniston where the day was completed by train to rejoin the main line for the journey home. The cost of such excursions was about seven shillings and six pence.

Such expense was beyond the means of most working class families and these excursions were usually organised by employers as a 'treat' for their workforce or by Sunday Schools for their annual outing. One would not expect much irresponsible behaviour from such groups and although the *Westmorland Gazette* reported incidents where day-trippers from Jarrow had harassed other visitors and a few over-excited members of a Sunday

Keswick Station Hotel.

School party had raided private gardens to steal plants and flowers, these seem to have been rare examples of misconduct and for the most part these tourists were well-behaved and did little to justify the gloomy predictions of Ruskin and Wordsworth.[7]

The rapid construction of well-appointed station hotels (Windermere 1847, Furness Abbey 1847, Grange-over-Sands 1866, Keswick 1869) to accommodate those tourists who could afford to stay there is an indication that it was not the 'lower classes' who featured in the calculations of railway directors. Indeed, in the early years, the railway companies made no provision for carrying 'the very lowest order of persons' but eventually allowed freight contractors to accept 'persons in the lower stations of life'.

The carriages provided for this purpose were described as 'very like a rabbit hutch'. The advertisements devised by the hoteliers were aimed at a clientele of comfortable wealth and ambitious social aspirations: The Old England Hotel at Bowness claimed to be 'Patronized by the Aristocracy and Elite of American Tourists'; the Crown Hotel at Windermere was 'Patronized by Royalty, American Presidents and the Rothschilds'; the Royal Oak at Keswick claimed the patronage of HRH the Prince of Wales, the King of Saxony and other Distinguished Visitors'; the Derwentwater Hotel announced its respectability by claiming a clientele of 'Families of Distinction'.[8]

The visitors lists published each week in the local press point clearly to the predominance of well-heeled northern tourists with a small number from the southern counties, from Bristol, Ireland and the United States. Vacation reading parties which usually included a number of rock-climbing enthusiasts from Oxford and Cambridge Universities were also beginning to make regular summer visits. All the evidence would seem to support the conclusion reached by two modern historians that 'Lakeland, despite excursion trains and "round trips" provided by the Furness and

Cloudsdale's Crown Hotel, Windermere, advertisement, 1880

other railways, tended to attract middle-class holiday-makers rather than the masses.'[9]

One often overlooked aspect of Lakeland tourism after the arrival of the railways at Windermere and Keswick is the stimulus given to the coach trade. In most parts of England the rapid construction of railway lines brought the era of the stage-coach to an end and many of the fine coaching inns fell on hard times, but in the Lake District the railheads could be some distance from the central tourist area and enterprising hoteliers began to operate their own coach services.

They also kept coaches for hire at a cost of £1 a day for a one-horse carriage with an additional five shillings a day for the driver.[10] The 1849 *Mannex Directory for Westmorland* contained the information that coaches from Windermere Railway Station ran daily to Keswick, Cockermouth, Hawkshead and other destinations. The Windermere to Keswick journey was in great demand even at a cost of seven shillings for an outside seat (nine shillings to travel inside) for the 24 miles. The three to four hour journey on a rutted and pot-holed road could be a thrilling (or terrifying) experience as coach-drivers competed to cover the distance in as short a time as possible.

This service continued until 1920, a sure indicator that the coming of the railway to Windermere in 1847 did not sound the death knell of the stage-coach as far as Lakeland was concerned; on the contrary, for at least 50 years it brought a period of unexpected prosperity. The principal operator of coach services was the Rigg family of the Windermere Hotel who by the end of the century owned fifteen coaches and kept 150 horses to pull them. Other hoteliers operated on a smaller scale catering for the tourist predilection for organised 'round trips' such as the Buttermere Round from Keswick through Borrowdale and over Honister Pass to Buttermere, where a leisurely lunch was taken at the Fish Inn,

Advertisement poster for Rigg's Coach Services.

before the return journey via Newlands Valley arriving in Keswick in time for evening dinner.

The experience of passing through so much magnificent scenery on this trip was accompanied by the thrill of the steep ascents and descents: the former passengers had to disembark from the coach or wagonette and walk – or sometimes push. This was probably the most popular tourist excursion in the Lake District and also the cheapest at five shillings, with an extra one shilling for the boat fare across Crummock Water to visit Scale Force.

A quite different expedition was recommended in Black's *Picturesque Guide to the English Lakes*: the coach left Keswick at 8.30am and arrived at Seathwaite in Borrowdale one and a half hours later. Here the men left the coach to begin a walk over Styhead to Wasdale Head where lunch was served at 12 noon. An hour later the walk continued via Black Sail Pass and Scarth Gap and so to the inn at Buttermere at 4.45pm. This excursion was considered to be far too strenuous for the ladies who had been left behind at Seathwaite to proceed in the coach over Honister Pass to spend the day at Buttermere. All enjoyed a meal at the inn and left at 6.30pm for a run through the Vale of Lorton before returning to Keswick at 8.30pm.

There was, it seems, a much greater diversity among the tourists who came to the Lake District as the ease of travel by rail began to have its effect. The largely wealthy and educated upper classes who had 'discovered' Lakeland in the eighteenth and early nineteenth centuries, and had come in search of the picturesque, were soon to be outnumbered by the equally well-to-do but rather less 'cultured' middle-class from the newly developing industrial towns of the northern counties and the Midlands who came for a holiday, a change of environment, fresh air and the personal uplift which the mountain scene could inspire.

They were not explorers or pioneers and were keen to patronise the organised excursions and diversions arranged for them. Either by accident or design there was little development of commercial amusements: the capital outlay was not justified by the return expected from so short a season and from a clientele who came just at weekends. Many visitors preferred sightseeing, walking, rowing on the lake or a quiet day fishing. There was a small group, a select minority, mainly from the universities but also from the professions of law, education, medicine and the church, – a class which, it has been suggested, 'formed a kind of bridge between the aristocracy and the middle class'[11] – and they were among the first visitors who came to the Lakes with the primary purpose of climbing the fells and conquering the crags.

A number of sprightly young ladies from the same social background such as Eliza Lynn Linton and Mary Elizabeth Braddon also came to walk the fells and scale the summits which had struck such memorable terror into the hearts of their eighteenth century predecessors. Fell-walking and rock-climbing did not

Early fell walkers.

become a popular tourist activity until late in the century follow-ing the publication of detailed guidebooks such as Murray's *Handbook to the Lakes* (1867) and M. J. B. Baddeley's classic *Thorough Guide to The English Lake District* (1886).

It is doubtful if the 'uneducated masses' had quite the negative effect on the peace and tranquillity of the area that Wordsworth had anticipated, except perhaps in tourist 'hot-spots' such as Keswick and Bowness and then only on summer weekends and, after 1871, the new Bank Holidays. John Ruskin's agonised plea: 'I do not want to let them see Helvellyn while they are drunk' was probably misplaced.

According to Beatrix Potter it was the local 'roughs' who caused trouble through over indulgence in drink. For the great majority of these 'plebian' tourists their day in the Lake District was a brief respite from the dreary ten-hour working days in the noise and dirt of the factory, mill or mine and from the cramped squalor of the long streets of terraced housing where they lived. For most of these folk their day in the countryside would be made memorable by a steamer trip on the lake, the spectacle of a Regatta, the competitive excitement of wrestling matches and sailing events, the colourful displays of fireworks, the cannon-fire echoes, or a family picnic on the lake and the special treat of ice-cream. Visitors to Keswick and Bowness would find such tourist amenities in place by the middle of the century and, for those whose recreational needs lay in other directions, there was usually a posse of prostitutes from West Cumberland.[12]

By the middle decades of the nineteenth century the Lake District had acquired a number of quality hotels and an adequate supply of homely farmhouse accommodation for visitors, but the towns were still woefully lacking in provision for those who wished to stay there. Windermere (Birthwaite) was still a small hamlet with a population of less than 500 and had a few lodging houses, but Bowness was rapidly becoming a place of villas hidden in shrubberies with a scattering of modest hotels and lodging houses.

The thousands of excursionists who descended on Windermere station were day-trippers and only appeared in large numbers at the Whitsuntide holiday: they did not come to stay. Indeed Windermere in the last decades of the nineteenth century has been described as 'a select residential resort'[13], a description which might aptly be applied to both Ambleside and Keswick where, except for incursions of day-trippers on a few summer weekends, visitors were mainly from the professional or upper and affluent middle classes who came to stay for several weeks. Even so these resorts seem to have been ill-prepared to receive them: Harriet Martineau writing of Ambleside in mid-Victorian times commented that 'there are no baths in the place; a simple deficiency where there is so much of company on the one hand and of water on the other'; she also referred to shortages of milk and other foods in the summer season 'when the district is most thronged with strangers'.

Keswick was the subject of a damning report by a civil engineer, Robert Rawlinson, who in 1852 condemned out of hand the appalling provision there for sewage disposal, water supply and the general sanitary state of the town: apart from 'one long street of good houses ... houses and tenements are crowded with foul middens and are encroached upon by privies, with large open cesspools, by pigsties, stables, cowsheds, and by slaughter houses' from all of which pollution drained away into the soil or into the River Greta from which many inhabitants drew their water.[14]

Rawlinson's report spurred the citizens of Keswick into immediate action and by the time the railway began to bring more tourists into the area the town had been transformed, so much so that at the turn of the century Baddeley's 'Guide' carried the information that 'Except for a few nights at one or more of the comfortable inns which stand in Borrowdale and on the margins of the wild western lakes, it is Keswick or nowhere.'

In any attempt to assess the impact of the railways on the Lake District in the mid-nineteenth century it is helpful to study the census returns of the time. The adult male population of England was calculated at about eight and a half million; of these less than a quarter of a million fell within the definition of 'middle class' and of these the overwhelming majority declared their income to be under £300 per annum. This has to be compared with the average wages of the unskilled industrial worker which were rarely more than ten shillings a week; a skilled worker could earn three or even four times this sum, but the expense of a family holiday or even a day excursion to the Lake District was beyond most working class budgets in the mid-nineteenth century.

It is true that by the 1860s most food commodities were much cheaper and these workers were consequently slightly better off but the depression of the 1870s was to demonstrate just how fragile was the economy of a working class household. Apart from a rare sponsored excursion there was little possibility of these 'masses' over-running the Lake District or any other holiday destination. In 1850, here as elsewhere in Britain, it was overwhelmingly the middle classes who were able to take advantage of the ease of travel brought by the railways.

Thomas Cook's cheap weekend excursions may have helped hundreds of working class families to enjoy their first sight of Lake Windermere or Skiddaw, but it was to be many decades before first the bicycle and a country bus service which we can now only envy, and then the introduction of holidays with pay, gave the 'humbler ranks of society' the opportunity and the means to make a significant impact on the tourist economy and the 'tourist culture' of the Lake District. Certainly in the mid-nineteenth century tourists were overwhelmingly upper or middle class but unlike their predecessors a century earlier they did not come primarily in search of the picturesque; they were 'holiday makers first, sightseers second, devotees of romantic mountain solitude hardly at all.'[15]

The coming of the railways may have increased the number of tourists visiting the Lake District but even by the end of Victoria's reign the impact on the landscape and life of the area was insignificant. Wordsworth could not have foreseen that the motor car rather than the railway would be far more effective in 'transferring uneducated persons in large bodies to particular spots' and bring not a few thousand but 20 million tourists every year to Lakeland.

12

OH! THAT WE HAD A BOOK OF BOTANY

THE change in attitude to wild and mountainous countryside which overwhelmed educated society between 1650 and 1750 also applied to nature in a wider sense. Animals, birds and insects continued to be indiscriminately slaughtered in vast numbers in accordance with the 'vermin' Statutes of Tudor times and any plant which was not known to traditional herbal medicine was eradicated as a pernicious weed, but there was a rapidly growing sense that the natural world should be studied for its own sake and appreciated as an enhancement of human life. From the wide-ranging studies of John Ray at the end of the seventeenth century to the detailed engravings of Thomas Bewick and the 36 volumes of Smith and Sowerby's *English Botany* there was a remarkable and unprecedented flood of work on all aspects of natural history.[1]

The Cumbrian-born botanist, Peter Collinson, commented in 1747 that books on natural history 'sell the best of any books in England'. Six hundred books on botany and horticulture were published in the course of this century and many English counties could boast a study of their own flora, while John Abercrombie's *Every Man his own Gardener* went through sixteen editions between 1767 and 1800. Natural history, and botany in particular, had become the fashionable pastime of the Georgian age, an enthusiasm given additional impetus by King George III, recognised throughout Europe as a keen, competent and scientific botanist. Country clergy and middle class ladies were prominent in the search for plants and, armed with a pocket guide to the Linnean

Classification, they walked the fields and woodlands recording every plant they discovered.

Alpine Lady's Mantle.

The Lake District, remote and virtually unknown, did not feature in this frenzy of botanical studies. There was no county *Flora* for either Cumberland or Westmorland - hence Dorothy Wordsworth's *cri de coeur* 'Oh! that we had a book of botany' to help her give names to all the flowers and plants she came across in her observant walks. In her *Grasmere Journal* she refers to numerous flowers by name but admits there were 'some others whose names I do not yet know'.[2] She died thirty years before J. G. Baker published his *Flora of the Lake District*.

It was often the ladies who were most involved in the contemporary passion for botanising. These lady tourists were not daytrippers; they came for several weeks or even longer and one wonders how they spent all the hours when they were abandoned while the gentlemen set off on their 'dangerous' walks into the mountains. It is not too fanciful to imagine that they roamed the woods and valley fields noting all the plants, flowers, mosses, ferns and lichens which grew so prolifically. Plant collecting as well as plant recording was the accepted custom at that time; Dorothy Wordsworth frequently notes how she managed to 'take up roots' and 'take home a great load'. One hopes that not too many botanical tourists followed her example.[3]

One 'tourist' who had a keen eye for the botanical riches of the Lake District was Eliza Lynn Linton whom we last met scaling the crags of Riggindale. Her account of her tour of the Lakes – *The Lake Country* – has an appendix listing several hundred plants of all kinds with both their Latin and their common names and the sites where they were to be seen. (Her list of ferns and mosses was borrowed from a similar list compiled by Harriet Martineau for her *Complete Guide to the Lakes* just a few years earlier).

Bird's Eye Primrose, above, and Mountain Avens, courtesy of Friends of the Lake District, below.

The Wild Cat by Thomas Bewick. Most guide books of the late 18th century refer to the wild cat as a common inhabitant of the woods and crags of the Lake District at that time. There were few, if any, remaining by the mid-19th century.

That the authors of Lake District guides should include such detailed information about the botany of the area is a useful indicator that many tourists of the time were keen botanists, happy to spend many hours enjoying familiar and discovering unfamiliar species in the mountain landscape. A portable press for preserving their specimens would, no doubt, be part of their 'essential' holiday luggage, specimens later used by some of those enthusiasts to produce portfolios of botanical paintings and drawings. Jane Loudon, the distinguished Victorian botanist, believed that 'to be able to draw flowers botanically is one of the most useful accomplishments of ladies of leisure'.

A flavour of the enthusiasm of these amateur botanists is portrayed in two passages written by Eliza Lynn Linton, one practical and restrained describing the difficulties facing plant-hunters on Honister Crag, the other a lyrical description of the flora near Buttermere:

At the base of the crag are broad tracts of alpine ladies' mantle (*alchemilla alpina*), while forked spleenwort (*asplenium septentrionale*) and many a rare plant beside, are to be found among the screes and shelving sides; in places not always easily accessible, certainly; but courage and patience do a great deal towards filling the pockets of a plant collector.[4]

Belts of blue lobelia are round Buttermere Lake, and great purple spikes of loosestrife are in the meadows, and the air is full of the scent of meadowsweet, and the hedges are yellowed with the yellow vetch, and the fields and lanes are gold-spotted with the hawkweed tribe; and down by that sweetly-singing Mill Beck grow blue forget-me-nots and still bluer birdlime, and all manner of wild plants and pleasant herbs.[5]

There were few, if any, professional botanists studying the flora of Cumberland and Westmorland, but botanising was undoubtedly the characteristic pastime of the ladies of the gentry and middle class in these years. The Lake District would have been an almost unexplored happy hunting ground for these amateur

The Golden Eagle by Thomas Bewick. Eighteenth century writers also refer |to the presence of both the Golden Eagle and the Sea Eagle in many areas of the Lake District but their numbers were being rapidly reduced by persecution and the last eagles were recorded in the middle years of the nineteenth century.

enthusiasts; their tour to the Lake District would have been as memorable for the discovery and identification of alpine flora and other plants peculiar to the northern regions of the country as for all the splendours of the 'picturesque' scenery and the thrills and 'horrors' of the precipitous crags and the frightful abyss.

One wonders if they also found excitement in the sight of the golden eagle floating high above their heads or ventured too close to the dens of the wild cats which, as the guidebooks warned, were 'fierce and daring animals' and 'inhabit in too great plenty these woods and rocks'. To the tourist from the southern counties, even to the most dedicated botaniser, the sight of such awesome creatures must have been as momentous an occasion as the discovery of a bird's eye primrose or the even rarer mountain avens.

REFERENCES

Chapter One

1. A, Young, *A Six Months Tour Through the North of England, 1770. Vol. 3,* p113.
2. Daniel Defoe, *A Tour Through the Whole Island of Great Britain,* ed. G. D. H. Cole, 1927, p678-88.
3. James Clarke, *A Survey of the Lakes of Cumberland, Westmorland and Lancashire,* 1787, p37; William Hutchinson, *An Excursion to the Lakes in Westmorland and Cumberland,* 1773-4, p171-2; William Wordsworth, *Guide to the Lakes,* ed. E. de Setincourt. 1970, p45.
4. Ralph Thoresby, *The Diary of Ralph Thoresby,* ed. J. Hunter, 1850, Vol.1, p267, (quoted in Keith Thomas, *Man and the Natural World,* 1983, p258).
5. Celia Fiennes, *The Journeys of Celia Fiennes,* ed. C. Morris, 1947, pp195, 198. Sarah Aust, *A Companion and Useful Guide to the Beauties of Scotland and the Lakes,* 1796, p19. Grevil Lindop, *A Literary Guide to the Lake District,* 1993, p122.
6. John Norden, *The Surveyors Dialogue,* 1607, p107, (quoted in Keith Thomas, *Religion and the Decline of Magic,* 1973, p195). J. E. C Hill, *Puritans and the Dark Corners of the Land, TRHSxiii,* 1963, (quoted in Keith Thomas, *ibid,* p196).
7. John Murray, *Handbook to Cumberland, Westmorland and the Lakes,* 1867.
8. Browne MSS, *Westmorland Record Office, Vol. 1,* p220. Arthur Young, *op. cit. Vol.4,* p430.
9. William Rollinson, *History of Cumberland and Westmorland,* 1978, p89.
10. K. Thomas, *Man and the Natural World,* 1983, p280.

Chapter Two

The following works contain much useful information about the roads of the Lake District in the 18th and 19th centuries:

1. P. Hindle, *Roads and Tracks of the Lake District,* 1998; L.A. Williams, *Road Transport in Cumbria in the 19th century,* 1975; W. Albert, *The Turnpike Road System in England 1660-1840,* 1972; C. M. L. Bouch,

Prelates and People of the Lake Counties, 1948; J. Stockdale, Annals of Cartmel, 1822; J. F. Curwen, Records of Kendal III, 1926.

Details of the coaching era in the Lake District may be found in the following:

2. *W. Wilson, Coaching in Lakeland. 1885; J. M. Carnie, At Lakeland's Heart, 2002; Blacks Picturesque Guide to the English Lakes, 1841.*

3. *Mary Maria Higginson, Holidays in Lakeland, England, 1831-32 (reference in J. Marshall, Old Lakeland, 1971, p168).*

The following books contain much interesting detail concerning the route across the sands of Morecambe Bay:

4. *J. Lofthouse, The Curious Traveller: Lancaster to Lakeland, 1956; T. Pape, The Sands of Morecambe Bay, 1947; P. Hindle, op. cit. p115-122; C. Robinson, Sandman of Morecambe Bay, 1989.*

5. *For details of some of the disasters on the sands route see C. Robinson, op. cit. p31-2.*

6. *'Lakers' – A name given to the early tourists and defined in the European Magazine in 1798 as 'those persons who visit the beautiful scenes in Cumberland and Westmorland by distinction styled the Lakes.'*

Chapter Three

1. *K. Thomas, Man and the Natural World, 1983, p260.*

2. *A Claude glass was a plain convex glass, 4 to 4.5 inches in diameter with a black foil for sunny days and a silver foil for cloudy days. Viewers turned their backs on the view and the mirror presented an image of the scene reduced to the size of a picture – hence the term 'picturesque'.*

3. *J. Budworth, A Fortnight's Ramble to the Lakes in Westmorland, Lancashire and Cumberland, 1792, p271.*

4. *Not eveiyone approved of young ladies prying into the 'private parts' of flowers and plants. John Ruskin considered that 'the gentle and happy scholar of flowers' would have 'nothing whatever to do with these obscene processes and prurient apparitions' (quoted in K. Thomas, op. cit. p65-6)*

5. *S. Watson, The Reign of George III, 1960, (Oxford History of England), p523.*

6. *H. Mayhew, London Labour and the London Poor, 1851. Selections ed. Peter Quennell, 1969, p23.*

7. *J. S. Mill, Principles of Political Economy, 1848, Vol.iv, Book 6.2 (quoted in K. Thomas, op. cit. p268-9). W. Pearson, Letters, Journals and Notes on the Natural History of Lyth, passim. W. Gilpin, Observations Chiefly*

Relative to Picturesque Beauty, 1786, i, p7-8.

8. W. Gilpin, op.cit. Vol ii p44.

9. W Hutchinson, An Excursion to the Lakes in Westmorland, &c, 1776, p191.

10. N. Nicholson, The Lakers, the First Tourists, 1955, p64.

11. J. Austen, Pride and Prejudice, Chapter XXVII.

12. P. Hindle, Roads and Trackways of the Lake District, 1984, Chapter 5.

Chapter Four

1. D. Ogg, Europe of the Ancien Regime, Collins, 1965, p350.

2. N. Gash, Aristocracy and People, Britain 1815-65, Arnold, p17-20,1979.

3. A. Foreman, Georgiana, Duchess of Devonshire, Harper Collins, 1998, p10.

4. ibid, p11.

5. Dorothy Wordsworth, Grasmere Journals, 8 June 1800.

6. P. Bicknell and R. Woof, The Lake District Discovered, 1983, passim.

7. T. K. Derry and T. L. Williams, A Short History of Technology, Oxford, 1960, p650.

8. William Green's Exhibition Galleries in Keswick and Ambleside attracted many visitors. John Briggs was enthusiastic and noted in his journals 'At the head of those things which excited in my bosom the most lively sensation I would most certainly place Mr Green's Exhibition of Views of the Lakes': (Remains of John Briggs 1825). Ellen Weeton refers to the same exhibition frequently in her Journal of a Governess (1809), but complains of the high prices and the one shilling admission charge, probably justifiably as the modem equivalent would be about £5.

9. Dorothy Wordsworth, Letter to S. T. Coleridge, 6 March, 1804.

10. P. Bicknell and R. Woof, The Discovety of the Lake District, 1983.

11. William Gilpin, Observations on the River Wye, 1782, p18.

12. William Gilpin, Observations Relative Chiefly to Picturesque Beauty... on the Mountains and Lakes of Cumberland and Westmorland, 1786, i. p127.

13. William Combe and Thomas Rowlandson, The Tour of Dr Syntax in Search of the Picturesque, 1812.

14. J. S. Mill, Principles of Political Economy, 1848, (Vol.iv, Book 6.2. 1965 edition).

15. William Wordsworth. Lines composed ...above Tin tern Abbey, 1798, 1.37.

Chapter Five

1. *William Mason, The Works of Thomas Gray Esq. 1827, p299, quoted in Grevel Lindop, A Literary Guide to the Lake District, 1993, p46; Sarah Anst, A Companion and Useful Guide to the Beauties of Scotland and the Lakes, 1799, p19.*

2. *H. D. Rawnsley, Literary Associations of the English Lakes, 1901, Vol.11 p60; Mary Moorman, William Wordsworth, A Biography, 1965, Vol.11 p222; E. Linton, The Lake Country, 1864, p132-3.*

3. *Joseph Budworth, A Fortnight's Ramble to the Lakes in Westmorland, Cumberland and Lancashire, 1792, pp100, 65-6; The Notebooks of Samuel Taylor Coleridge, ed. K. Coburn, p1225, quoted in G. Lindop, op.cit. p358.*

4. *John Briggs, Letters from the Lakes, 1825, p174-6.*

5. *Ronald Sands, The Wordsworth Country, 1984, pi18. Celia Fiennes, The Illustrated Journeys, ed. C. Morris, 1982, p165-6. Arthur Young, A Six Months Tour through the North of England, 1770, Vol.III, p591.*

6. *F. W. Garnett, Westmorland Agriculture 1800-1910, 1912, p8; Dorothy Wordsworth, Journals, ed. E. de Selincourt, 1941, Vol.1 p97; Joseph Budworth, op. cit. p289-90.*

7. *Sarah Aust, op. cit. p19; James Clarke, A Survey of the Lakes of Cumberland, Westmorland and Lancashire, 1797, p84-6; Thomas Gray, Journal in the Lakes, 1775, p28.*

8. *Joseph Budworth, op. cit. p65-6.*

9. *ibid. pp197, 201-2.*

10. *Harriet Martineau, A Complete Guide to the English Lakes, 1858, p50.*

11. *H. D. Rawnsley, op. cit. Vol. II, p227; E. L. Linton, op. cit. p129.*

12. *John Keats, Letters, Vol. I, p307, quoted in G. Lindop, op. cit. p153.*

Chapter Six

1 *Fit for the Future: Report of the National Parks Review Panel, 1991, p8.*

2. *W. Gilpin, Observations on the Mountains and Lakes of Cumberland and Westmorland, 1786, i, p7.*

3. *W. Gell, A Tour in the Lakes made in 1797, ed. W. Rollinson, 1968, p14.*

4. *J. Clarke, A Survey of the Lakes... 1787, p94.*

5. *ibid. p64-5.*

6. *W. Hutchinson, An Excursion to the Lakes... 1776 (1786 edn), p65-7*

7. *R. Southey, Letters from England... Don Espriell, ed. J. Simmons, 1951, p243.*

8. S, Aust (Hon. Mrs Murray), A Companion and Useful Guide, 1796, p21-2.

9. J. Budworth, A Fortnight's Ramble to the Lakes, 1792, p210.

10. R. Southey, op.cit. p238.

11. W. Gilpin, op.cit. i, p209.

12. G. J. Symonds, The Floating Island of Derwentwater, 1888.

13. A. Burl, The Stone Circles of the British Isles, 1976. p56 et seq.; J. Waterhouse, Stone Circles of Cumbria, 1985, p45; W. Mason, The Works of Thomas Gray, 1827, p295-7.

14. Quoted in G. Bott: Keswick, the Story of a Lake District Town 1994, p3.

Chapter Seven

1. Norman Nicholson, The Lakers, (1955), p67.

2. Wordsworth noted in his own Guide (p6 footnote) that 'Mr Green's Guide to the Lakes, in two vols., contains a complete Magazine of minute and accurate information.'

3. Joseph Budworth, A Fortnight's Ramble to the Lakes, (1792), p271; Edward Baines, Companion to the Lakes, 1829, p218 (1834 ed.); Ellen Weeton. Journal of a Governess 1809-11, p274 (1936); Black's Picturesque Guide to the Lakes, 1841, p138 (1870 ed).

4. Charles Lamb, Letters, quoted by Norman Nicholson, The Lake District, An Anthology, 1978, p252-4.

5. Robert Southey, quoted by R. Sands, The Wordsworth Country, 1984, p119-20.

6. John Ruskin, Iteriad, 1830, ed. J. S. Dearden & V. A. James, 1969, p20 etseq.; Charles Lamb, v. supra.; Eliza Lynn Linton, The Lake Country, 1864, p94; Edward Baines, op.cit. p211 et seq.

7. S. T. Coleridge, Tour in the Lake County, 1802, quoted in N. Nicholson, The Lakers, p43-5. (Alan Hankinson's 'Coleridge Walks the Fells Ellenbank 1991, is a beautifully written account of the poet's adventure.)

8. W. Wordsworth, The Somnambulist; see also D. Robertson and P. Koronka, Secrets and Legends of Old Westmorland, 1992, p135.

9. Budworth, op.cit. p215; E. L. Linton, op.cit. p190-1; William Cell, A Tour in the Lakes Made in 1797, ed. . Rollinson, 1968, p11; J. S. Mill, Works, XXVII, p520, (quoted by G. Lindop, A Literary Guide to the Lake District, 1993, p58).

11. Dorothy Wordsworth, George and Sarah Green, a Narrative, ed. E. de Selincourt, 1936.

12. James Clarke, A Survey of the Lakes, 1787, p118.

13. *A Westmorland Notebook, 1889, p263.*

14. *Quoted in The Lake District Discovered 1810-50 by Peter Bicknell and Robert Woof, 1982, p263, Trustees of Dove Cottage.*

15. *William Wilson, Coaching in Lakeland, 1885, p23.*

16. *A. Burl, the Stone Circles of the British Isles, 1976, p.56 seq.*

17. *W. Hutchinson, History of the County of Cumberland, 1794, Vol I, p419-20.*

18. *Harriet Martineau, A Complete Guide to the English Lakes, 1858, (E. P. Publishing, 1974 ed, p25-6, (1858 ed. p 91).*

19. *John Wyatt, Reflections on the Lakes, 1980, p178-81.*

20. *Thomas West, Guide to the Lakes, 1778, p64; William Gilpin, Observations on the Mountains and Lakes of Cumberland and Westmorland, 1786, p135, 138-9; William Gell, op.cit., p11.*

21. *A. C. Gibson, The Old Man...or Ravings and Ramblings, 1854, p34-5; see also H. Martineau, op.cit., p115-6.*

22. *Quoted from Coleridge's Notebooks in G. Lindop, op. cit., p327.*

Chapter Eight

1. *Jane Austen, Pride and Prejudice, Chapter VII.*

2. *Dorothy Wordsworth, Journals, ed. E. de Selincourt, 1941, Vol. I, p427-30.*

3. *Dorothy Wordsworth, The Grasmere Journal, 9 June 1800.*

4. *William Green, The Tourists New Guide, 1818, Vol. I, p322*

5. *Elizabeth Gaskell, Life of Charlotte Bronte, Everyman, 1973, p309.*

6. *Letters of Charles and Mary Lamb, ed. E. H. Marrs, Vol. II, p69: Edward Baines, A Companion to the Lakes, 1834, p211 seq.: John Barrow, Mountain Ascents, 1888, p94.*

7. *Dorothy Wordsworth, The Grasmere Journal, 25 October, 1801*

8. *Thomas Wilkinson, Tours to the British Mountains, 1824, pp169, 98-100.*

9. *Ellen Weeton, Journal of a Governess 1809-11, 1936, p272-4.*

10. *ibid. p249, 294.*

11. *Eliza Lynn Linton, The Lake Country, 1864, pp 49, 35, 37-8.*

12. *ibid. pp129, 196-7.*

13. *ibid.pp18, 30, 190-1.*

14. *Sarah Aust, (The Hon. Mrs Murray), A Companion and Useful Guide to the Beauties of Scotland and the Lakes, 1799, p19.*

15. *Linton op. cit., pp18, 30, 190-1.*

16. *ibid. pp42, 98, 86.*

17. *ibid, p134-5.*
18. *ibid. p49.*
19. *ibid. p205.*
20. *ibid. p210.*
21. *ibid. p211-2.*

Chapter Nine

1. *William Wordsworth, Guide to the Lakes, 1835, ed. E. de Selincourt, 1935, p72.*
2. *ibid, p70.*
3. *Ellen Weeton, Journal of a Governess 1809-11, OUP, 1936, p289.*
4. *Ronald Sands, The Wordsworth Country, 1984, p37-40.*
5. *Mrs Humphry Ward, A Writer's Recollections, Collins, 1918, p23-4.*
6. *Norman Nicholson, The Lakers, 1955, p102.*
7. *Robert Gambles, The Story of the Lakeland Dales, 1997, p131-2 and references.*
8. *Steven Watson, The Reign of George III, 1959, p338-9.*
9. *Quoted by Amanda Foreman, Georgiana Duchess of Devonshire, 1999, p35.*
10. *Jane Austen, Sense and Sensibility, 1811, Chapter X.*
11. *Thomas De Quincey, Reminiscences of the Lake Poets, Everyman edition, 1961, p34.*
12. *Dorothy Wordsworth, Grasmere Journal, 31 August 1800.*
13. *Robert Southey, Letters from England, ed. J. Simmons, 1951, p243.*
14. *Thomas De Quincey, op.cit. p205-6 and footnote.*
15. *J. D. Marshall, Old Lakeland, 1971, Chapter 7, Travellers Abroad, p126.*
16. *I am indebted to Grevel Lindop's encyclopaedic study A Literary Guide to the Lake District, 1993, for much of the detail of this section.*

Chapter Ten

1. *Quoted in Steven Watson, The Reign of George III, Oxford 1960, p13.*
2. *Thomas Short, An Essay towards a Natural Experimental and Medical History of the Principle Mineral Waters, Sheffield, 1740.*
3. *C. Kipling, The Borrowdale Salt Spring, Transactions of the Cumberland and Westmorland Antiquarian and Archaeological Society, Vol. I, xi, 1961.*
4. *William Hutchinson, A History of Cumberland, 1794, Vol. 1, p552.*
5. *The story of Scott's romantic meeting with Mary Carpenter at Gilsland is told by J. G. Lockhart in his Life of Scott, 1838, p74-9.*

6. *R. Alderson, A Chemical Analysis and Medical Treatise on the Shap Spa in Westmorland, 1828, pp16-22, 25-6.*
7. *Handbook to Shap Spa, 1850, p20.*

Chapter Eleven

1. *E.L. Woodward, The Age of Reform 1815-70, 1938, p39.*
2. *William Wordsworth, Letter to the Morning Post, 1844, Appendix II to Oxford 1970 edition of his Guide to the Lakes.*
3. *William Wordsworth, Second Letter to the Morning Post, (Appended Sonnet) ibid.*
4. *John Ruskin, Preface to Robert Somervell's Protest against the expansion of Railway in the Lake District.*
5. *George Bott, Keswick, The Story of a Lake District Town, 1994, p96.*
6. *Quoted in J. D. Marshall, Old Lakeland, 1971, p193.*
7. *J. D. Marshall and J. K. Walton, The Lake Counties from 1830 to the mid-twentieth century, 1981, p184-5. Reference: Westmorland Gazette, 25 August 1883.*
8. *J. D. Marshall, Old Lakeland, 1971, p180.*
9. *J. D. Marshall and M. Davies-Shiel, The Industrial Archaeology of the Lake Counties, 1969, p217.*
10. *Harriet Martineau, Complete Guide to the English Lakes, (3rd. edition), piii.*
11. *N. Gash, Aristocracy and People – Britain 1815-65, 1979, p22.*
12. *J. D. Marshall and J. K. Walton, op.cit, p188.*
13. *O. M. Westall, editor, Windermere in the 19th century, 1976, The Retreat to Arcadia: Windermere as a select residential resort in the late 19th century.*
14. *G. Bott, op.cit. p86-8.*
15. *J. D. Marshall and J. K. Walton, op.cit. p186.*

Chapter Twelve

1. *J. Ray, Synopsis Methodica Stirpium Britannicarum, 1690; T. Bewick, General History of Quadrupeds, 1790; History of British Birds, 1797-1804; J. Smith and J. Sowerby, English Botany, 36 volumes, 1790-1814.*
2. *D. Wordsworth, Grasmere Journal 1800-2, Oxford 1958, p24 and p166.*
3. *ibid, p162*
4. *E. Lynn Linton, The Lake Country, 1864, p198.*
5. *ibid, p193.*

ABOUT THE AUTHOR

ROBERT Gambles was born and grew up in Derbyshire. He was a scholar of St John's College, Oxford, where he took an Honours degree in Modern History and a post-graduate Diploma in Education. He also has a Licentiate Diploma in Music. His professional career was spent in Education, mainly in Ely and Liverpool.

He acquired a love of the Lake District early in life and he has lived in Cumbria in his years of retirement during which he has explored the whole district and written a number of books and many articles on various aspects of its history.

These have included *Man in Lakeland: 4,000 Years of Human Settlement; Out of the Forest: The Natural World and the Placenames of Cumbria; Walks around Windermere; The Place-names of the Yorkshire Dales; The Spa Resorts and Mineral Springs of Cumbria; Walks on the Borders of Lakeland; The Story of the Lakeland Dales* and *Echoes of Old Lakeland. Escape to the Lakes: The First Tourists* won an award at the 2012 Lake District Book of the Year event.

The author has also pursued his interest in a wider national history and a critical study of some of the well-known stories from British history was published in 2013 under the title *Great Tales from British History*, and was decribed by *The Guardian* as 'hugely enjoyable'. Through his Norwegian wife he acquired a special interest in the life and history of Norway.

A keen but pragmatic interest in conservation and the protection of the natural environment has always featured in his philosophy of life and he was for many years a Trustee and member of the Executive Committee of the Friends of the Lake District. He has also worked as a volunteer for the National Trust.

Books by Robert Gambles published by Hayloft:
Lake District Place Names,   (ISBN 978-1-904524-92-2)
Espen Ash Lad: Folk Tales from Norway,
                              (ISBN 978-1-910237-04-5)